A Guide to the Landscape Architecture of Boston

Jack Ahern

"What artist, so noble . . . who with far-reaching conception of beauty and designing power, sketches the outline, writes the colors, and directs the shadows of a picture so great that nature shall be employed upon it for generations . . ."

– Frederick Law Olmsted
"Walks and Talks of an American Farmer in England," 1852

The Hubbard Educational Trust
Cambridge, Massachusetts
1999

Dedication

This guidebook is dedicated to all those landscape architects that have worked for over a century to make Boston a more beautiful and healthy city. Their work has enriched the lives of generations of Bostonians.

The book is dedicated especially to all those who made earlier attempts to produce a guidebook to landscape architecture of Boston. Their ideas and research have contributed to the guide, and their spirit and passion for the profession has inspired its completion. Recognition and credit is due to Roger Erickson, Jestena Boughton, Lynn Wolff, and the Boston Society of Landscape Architects.

Jack Ahern

Preface

Over the last one hundred years Landscape Architects have made a significant contribution to the urban and suburban fabric of Boston and its environs. This guidebook is intended to share some of the more significant examples of Landscape Architecture on the occasion of the centennial celebration of the American Society of Landscape Architects in Boston in September 1999.

The works included in this guide are intended to help the public's understanding of the relationship between landscape architecture and the critical social and environmental issues of these and earlier times. As a historical review, this guide can also serve as a valuable tool for all students of the profession. Guidebooks reflecting works of landscape architecture are rare, making the realization of this work especially attractive to the Hubbard Educational Trust.

The mission of the Hubbard Educational Trust is to support projects that promote the profession by broadening and nourishing landscape architectural education. Founded in 1953 to honor Henry Vincent Hubbard, the co-author of *An Introduction to the Study of Landscape Architecture*, the Trust has supported oral and video histories, important publications, and the celebration of special people and places through its recognition awards.

Over the years, the Trust has sought out projects dealing with specific landscapes and landscape issues that might be used as models for preservation, education, and the promotion of Landscape Architecture. This guidebook is added to that long list of contributions to Landscape Architecture that the Hubbard Educational Trust is committed to support.

Hubbard Educational Trust, John Wacker, President

Boston Guidebook Committee
John F. Furlong
Carol R. Johnson
Marion Pressley
Lynn Wolff

April 1999

Boston Harbor Islands State Park

Table of Contents

Index Map

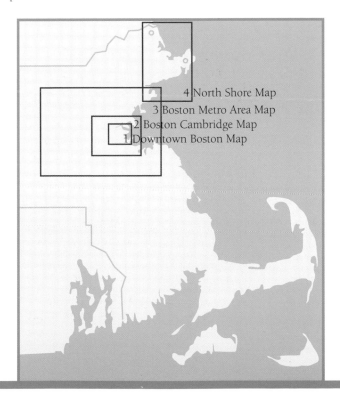

L andscape Architecture in Boston

A spectacular and diverse landscape and a rich cultural history uniquely characterize the city of Boston. The historical and contemporary works of landscape architecture in Boston hold as much significance as the city's place in American history and its world-renowned accomplishments in music, art, and architecture. Landscape architects in Boston have played a leading role in the development of the profession since its inception in the United States in the mid-nineteenth century. The first college program in landscape architecture was started here at Harvard. The city also lays claim to the first public park, the first arboretum, the first rural cemetery, and the first land trust. Today, Boston offers an unprecedented multiplicity of built works of landscape architecture including historic restoration, urban parks and civic spaces, waterfront redevelopment, transportation projects and greenways.

In the late nineteenth century, landscape architects Frederick Law Olmsted Sr. and Charles Eliot realized the importance of protecting the city's most significant natural resources - its rivers, harbor, beaches, neighborhood parks, and surrounding hills - as part of an effort to keep Boston's unique character and vitality. As a result Boston became the exemplar. These two men's influence extended to nearly every major American city. Protegees and students of Olmsted all across the country continue to provide innovative and visionary solutions to meet the ever-changing needs of the city and its people. Today's landscape architects are planning in advance, designing and building the landscapes of the future. Many of these yet-to-be-built projects in Boston are included in this guidebook such as the Central Artery (20) and the New Charles River Basin (33).

The Fens Victory Garden

Landscape architecture has many forms of expression in Boston, ranging from high-profile urban parks and civic spaces to protected areas that appear natural or untouched by humans. In addition to parks and squares, the unmistakable products of designers, this guidebook includes other projects that are less often identified as works of landscape architecture. Boston landscape architects have worked to prevent inappropriate uses of land and to protect and restore green corridors; see for example, Southwest Corridor Park (76) and Upper Charles River Greenway (145). Landscape architects regularly do restorations of natural ecological systems and try to conceal adverse man–made impacts, as can be seen at the Lower Neponset River Reservation (136) and the Mystic River Reservation (164). In the case of the well-known and much-loved Emerald Necklace (49) historic landscapes have been restored to honor the past and to meet the changing needs of Bostonians. With its long and rich history, Boston offers a unique laboratory for the restoration and adaptive reuse of built landscapes.

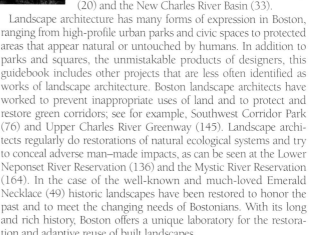

The Varieties of Built Works in Boston

Metropolitan Planning and Greenways

Landscape architects have strongly influenced the growth and development of Boston while protecting important and sensitive natural resources. Olmsted's Emerald Necklace (49) is an icon of international landscape architecture, inspiring generations of planners and designers throughout the world. Olmsted foresaw the importance of integrated open spaces and river corridors in the city, and his work demonstrates an uncanny ability to transform problems into cherished resources. Charles Eliot, a protegee of Olmsted, founded the world's first land trust, The Trustees of Reservations, and was instrumental in creating Boston's 1893 Metropolitan Open Space Plan. Much of the protected land that Boston now enjoys can be credited to the vision and effectiveness of these two men: Beaver Brook Reservation (147), Middlesex Fells (163), Blue Hills (138), Mystic River (164), Neponset River Reservations (136), and Revere Beach (174). The great tradition of greenway planning continues, and projects, such as the Upper Charles River Greenway (145), are transforming miles of riverfront from inappropriate uses and abuse into continuous healthy and beautiful river greenways.

(above) Downtown and the waterfront; (below) Cambridge and Downtown green areas

Waterfront, Riverfront and Harbor Islands

Boston has an intimate and evolving relationship with its waterfront and harbor as the city has been transformed from an industrial and commercial port into a vital urban resource for tourism, recreation, and cultural landscape restoration. Contemporary landscape architects, following the nineteenth-century vision of Olmsted and Eliot, are fully engaged in planning and designing this transformation, including restoration of the shoreline and development of landscapes with water-dependent commercial and residential uses. The Boston Redevelopment

Authority is creating a forty three-mile uninterrupted walk, nicknamed the Sapphire Necklace (69). Currently, about half of this walk is accessible around the perimeter of the harbor. The downtown section of the waterfront, Waterfront Park (7) and Long Wharf (8), was an early national model for urban waterfront restoration. The Charlestown Navy Yard continues the waterfront development with a number of successfully established projects (59,60,61). In East Boston, Piers Park (64) and the Harborwalk at Logan International Airport (65) provide harbor access and spectacular views of downtown. Boston Harbor is also unique in the

(above) Piers Park; (right) Dudley Town Common

world in that it has more islands near its downtown than any other city. Currently a major alliance of federal, state, city, and nonprofit groups is engaged in planning the development of tourism, recreation and natural area protection for the Boston Harbor Islands (131). Landscape architects are planning and designing many of these islands: Castle Island (74), Spectacle Island (132), Deer Island (133), and World's End (134). In addition, the Charles River Basin extends the city's waterfront around the downtown featuring the Esplanade (34) and the ambitious New Charles River Basin (33), a major riverfront restoration project associated with the Central Artery/Third Harbor Tunnel Project (20).

Civic Spaces

Great cities are defined as much by the character and quality of their civic spaces as they are by their architecture. Landscape architects have designed most of Boston's memorable civic spaces. The Back Bay's Copley Square (19), defined by some of the city's most distinguished architecture, was created in the nineteenth century and has been redesigned several times to meet the changing social and economic needs of the city. Nearby, the monumental urban landscape at the Christian Science Church's world headquarters (47) creates a powerful and memorable civic space featuring a six hundred seventy five-foot-long reflecting pool. Other notable civic spaces across the city include the Dudley Town Common in Roxbury (78) and in the

South End Harriet Tubman Park (43) that commemorates Tubman's important role in the underground railroad during the Civil War. In downtown Boston, Post Office Square Park (11) was built through an innovative public/private partnership with neighboring landowners on the site of a former parking garage. One of the newest civic spaces in Boston is the United States Federal Court House on Fan Pier (70), which provides harbor access and dramatic views of the harbor and of downtown.

Transportation

Boston's complex geography and Colonial-Era street pattern present immense challenges for modern transportation planning. Landscape architects have skillfully integrated new roads and transportation facilities into the city's urban fabric while at the same time providing efficiency and amenity. In the 1970's, a five-mile long transportation corridor was reconceived as the Southwest Corridor Park (76) and was, at that time, Boston's largest park project since the Emerald Necklace. More recently, Boston upgraded and expanded its transit system to include a number of new and redesigned rapid transit stations, often associated with important civic spaces: Harvard Square (106), Porter Square (150), and Davis Square (169). Landscape architects have designed a number of bikeways including one running from Davis Square to Alewife Station (170) and the Minute Man Bikeway (159). The Central Artery/Third Harbor Tunnel Project (20), unquestionably the largest transportation project in the nation's history, will create over thirty acres of new open space in downtown Boston.

Housing

The creation and redevelopment of successful multi-family housing presents the challenges of integrating landscape and building architecture within the surrounding city. In the South End, Tent City (42) was built in the 1980's as one of Boston's largest mixed-income housing projects. On the harborfront in Squantum, Marina Bay (140) is a mixed-use residential and commercial development, which provides a rich array of landscape amenities including an extensive boardwalk and a large marina. Different challenges are presented in revitalization projects for existing public housing including Orchard Park (81), Grant Manor (82), Harbor Point (84), Newtowne Court (124), and The Mystics (171). In these projects, landscape architects work with tenant organizations to reduce the negative effects of high density living while providing residents with private outdoor space and linkages with the community.

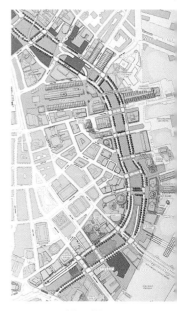

(Above) The existing Central Artery and (below) a section of the consensus plan

Commercial

The design of successful commercial facilities is a complex enterprise involving access, image, marketability, and adaptability. Landscape architects have contributed to the success of some of Boston's most notable commercial developments by providing

stimulating outdoor environments that attract people and integrate well into the neighborhood. Faneuil Hall, Quincy Market, and Marketplace Center (1) were developed as the first festival marketplace in the United States and it serves as a national model. It is also a fine example of adaptive reuse of historic structures. Downtown Crossing (17) and Shoppers' Park (13) provide a pedestrian-oriented environment in the downtown. Across the harbor, a number of projects at the Charlestown Navy Yard (59 - 61) transformed a derelict military facility into a vibrant office and commercial center with outstanding open space and harbor access. Lechmere Canal Park (125) is a newer project that extends the waterfront of the Charles River basin into the commercial center, creating a memorable open space. Outside the city, landscape architects are involved in developing successful office parks such as the Bay Colony Corporate Center (154) where steep topography, outstanding views, and innovative siting have created a model corporate campus.

Brownfields

Brownfields are contaminated sites, landfills, and other problem areas that were formerly declared off limits and forgotten. In brownfields restoration work, contemporary landscape architects are following F. L. Olmsted's tradition of finding the latent opportunity that lies hidden in any major environmental problem. Working on and leading interdisciplinary teams with engineers and scientists, landscape architects have shown that, in addition to toxic remediation, brownfields can be transformed into useful and beautiful parks and open spaces. Danahey Park in Cambridge (148) was built on a former landfill and now provides over twenty five percent of the public open space for the city of Cambridge. At the Mystic River Reservation (164), Arsenal Park (151) and Pope John Paul II Park (135), industrial debris was creatively used for surface restoration, creating an open space amenity while solving a challenging site disposal problem. In related work, excess fill from the Central Artery Project (20) was used to restore and recontour Gardner Street Park (101) and Spectacle Island (132). Brownfields restoration projects represent a new form of environmental stewardship, one in which the landscape architects' creative perspective, sensitivity to community concerns and technical skills play a particularly relevant and effective role.

Community Design
(Playgrounds, Schoolyards, and Community Gardens)

In socially diverse Boston, successful neighborhood design increasingly involves neighborhoods in the design process, creating a sense of community ownership and pride. A few notable examples of successful neighborhood park design include James Hayes Park (41), Doherty Playground (62), and Mozart Park (90). The Mayor of Boston's innovative Boston Schoolyard Initiative works with community groups, teachers, and students to transform public schoolyards into stimulating environments for learning and play. As part of this initiative the Warren Prescott Schoolyard (63) and the Hugh Roe O'Donnell Schoolyard (67) were transformed with educational plantings, children's art, and interpretive elements that linked these schoolyards with neighborhood history and the natural environment.

Community gardens provide yet another challenge to transform vacant or underused urban spaces into healthy productive gardens, that also serve a great social need. Funding is often severely limited for these gardens, and designers have learned to use salvaged and recycled materials to build special planters as at Forbes Street Community Garden (88) and Eagle Hill Memorial Community Garden (68).

Historic Restoration and Adaptive Re-use

Boston is both distinguished and challenged by its historic resources. This is true especially for the landscape, which presents perhaps the greatest challenge, since it is so changeable. Because of this challenge and the great concentration of landscape architects in the city, Boston has become a leading innovator in historic landscape restoration and adaptive reuse. The Massachusetts Department of Environmental Management (DEM), working with the National Park Service, coordinated the Olmsted Historic Restoration program by focusing political attention, research, and funding on the great Olmsted legacy in Boston. The program has completed many projects, most notably the Emerald Necklace Master Plan (64) and the restoration of most of the necklace parks and gardens (50 -57). The tradition is continuing with DEM's historic landscape preservation program for restoring historic landscapes throughout the entire state. Landscape architects have also designed adaptive reuse projects creating new uses in historic places while maintaining their essential link to history. Successful examples of adaptive reuse include the Charlestown Navy Yard (59 - 61), Faneuil Hall (1), and Long Wharf (8).

(above) Mozart Park spray wall; (below) Shipyard Park

Educational and Medical Institutions

Boston's medical institutions are world-renowned. Landscape architects have worked on most of these institutions as they have grown and changed to meet contemporary needs. The Longwood Medical Area, comprised of eighteen separate institutions, offers a unique opportunity to see the results of intelligent planning and skillful institutional design created over many years.

(above)
Northeastern
University; (below)
The Muddy River

Among the successful results are the designed landscapes evident at the Harvard Medical School Main Quadrangle (94), Longwood Medical Research Center (95), the Clinical Center at Beth Israel Hospital (96), New England Baptist Hospital Courtyards (97), the Children's Hospital Gateway Park and Winter Garden (98), and New England Deaconess Hospital (99). Landscape architects have also played major roles in the transformation of college and university campuses in the Boston Area. Northeastern University has been transformed into a pedestrian-friendly, urban campus environment in recent years (46). At Harvard University, the oldest college in the United States the focus of the campus is its historic yard (113) which contrasts markedly with the provocative and minimalist Tanner Fountain (114). Tufts University in Medford also has benefited from the skillful work of landscape architects at Bendetson Hall (165), the Meyer Campus Center (166) and the Tisch Family Library (167).

To best appreciate the true significance of Boston's built works, one must see them in person. The projects included in this guidebook have been selected to represent the full diversity of landscape architecture, including new and emerging areas of professional practice. The maps and project descriptions that follow will help you to find and enjoy all of these beautiful places in and around Boston. As you tour these sites, it will become clear that this old and active profession of landscape architecture has contributed to the health and quality of Boston's environment in a great variety of ways. The works that people enjoy today will inspire and educate the next generation of landscape architects, and it is they who will further build, transform and adapt the Boston environment into the next century and beyond.

Map 1 – Boston, Downtown

Project Index and Guide to Landscape Architecture Projects in Boston and the Boston Metropolitan Area

(above) Marketplace Center; (below) Museum of Fine Arts Japanese Garden

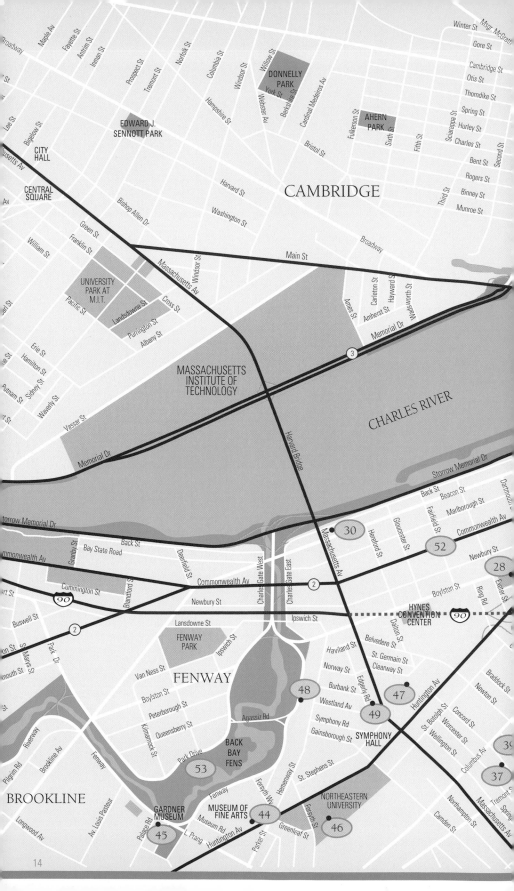

DOWNTOWN BOSTON
BEACON HILL
NORTH END
OLD NORTH CHURCH
CHINATOWN
BACK BAY
SOUTH END
SOUTH BOSTON
BOSTON COMMON
PUBLIC GARDENS
CITY HALL
FANEUIL HALL
PARK ST CHURCH
TRINITY CHURCH
FLEET CENTER/ NORTH STATION
FORT POINT CHANNEL
CAMBRIDGE GALLERIA
Main St
Rutherford Av
Msgr. O'Brien Hwy
Charles River Dam
Charlestown Bridge
Nashua St
Martha Rd
Lomasney Wy
Causeway St
Canal St
Friend St
Portland St
Traverse St
Merrimac St
Blossom St
Cardinal O'connell
Staniford St
New Chardon St
Fruit St
Parkman St
Grove St
Cambridge St
Longfellow Bridge
Phillips St
Revere St
Pinckney St
Cedar St
Mt. Vernon St
Chestnut St
Walnut St
Garden St
Irving St
Joy St
Myrtle St
Hancock St
Bowdoin St
Somerset St
Court St
Sudbury St
Congress St
Hanover St
North St
Clinton St
State St
Central St
India St
Water St
School St
Broomfield St
Milk St
Broad St
Battery March
Oliver St
Pearl St
High St
Franklin St
Winter St
Temple Pl
West St
Arch St
Otis St
Summer St
Chauncy St
Devonshire St
Federal St
Congress St
Purchase St
Atlantic Av
Mason St
Avery St
Av de Lafayette
Essex St
Kingston St
Park St
Beacon St
River St
Brimmer St
Charles St
Embankment Rd
Arlington St
Berkeley St
Clarendon St
Boylston St
Park Plaza
St. James Av
Stuart St
Melrose St
Fayette St
Columbus Av
Marginal St
Elliot St
Warrenton St
Charles St South
Tremont St
Lagrange St
Kneeland St
Harvard St
Hudson St
Lincoln St
Beach St
South St
Tyler St
Oak St
Atlantic Av
Dorchester Av
Congress St
Summer St
Northern
Herald St
Chandler St
Appleton St
Berkeley St
Tremont St
Clarendon St
Dartmouth St
Warren Av
Shawmut Av
Washington Av
Harrison Av
Berkeley St
Waltham St
Bristol St
Thayer St
4th St
Randolph St
Dedham St
Union St
Brookline St
Pembroke St
Newton St
Rutland St
Reynolds Wy
Park St
Malden St
Plympton St
Dedham St
Canton St
Albany St
Harrison Av
Dorchester Av
A St
W. Broadway
Commercial St
Prince St
Endicott St
Snowhill St
Charter St
Unity St
Washington St
Thatcher St
Cooper St
Margin St
Salem St
Cross St
Sheafe St
Tileston St
Bennet St
Battery St
Clark St
Fleet St
Hanover St
North St
New Atlantic Av
Commercial
Richmond St
Cross St
Sumner Tunnel (Toll)
Callahan Tunnel
Land Bl
Cambridge Pkwy
93
1
3
90
1 2 3 4 5 6 7 8 9 10 11 12 13 14 15 16 17 18 19 20 21 22 23 24 25 26 27 29 31 32 33 34 35 36 38 40 41 42 43 50 51
N
0 1/8 1/4 3/8 1/2 MILE
0 1/8 1/4 3/8 1/2 KILOMETER

*D*owntown Boston

This historic section of Boston was reborn as the first festival marketplace in the United States in 1976. Since then it has hosted over 200 million visitors. Over the past twenty years, Faneuil Hall Marketplace has served as a model and inspiration to major cities around the world. Traditional paving materials surround the buildings, performance areas and informal seating abound, and a memorable canopy of honey locusts encloses and shades the space, filtering the sunlight. Since their initial work on the project, Pressley Associates has upgraded, renovated, and expanded various parts of the marketplace. In 1985 Pressley designed the site for the adjacent Marketplace Center, an office and retail project that completed the Boston Redevelopment Authority's visionary *Walk to the Sea*, a continuous sequence of open space linking the Boston City Hall/Government Center complex with the waterfront. Marketplace Center has been recognized with an ASLA Urban Design Award in 1986, and a BSLA Urban Design Award in 1987. Faneuil Hall Marketplace received a National Landscape Award at the White House in 1979.

① **Faneuil Hall Marketplace & Marketplace Center**

Chatham, Clinton, and Commercial Streets

Pressley Associates

② **Custom House Plaza/ McKinley Square**

India, Central, and State Streets

Pressley Associates

Streetscape improvements to the historical Custom House and a new public plaza have helped to revitalize the area's urban environment while respecting the building's historical significance. The improvements are similar to those at nearby Faneuil Hall Marketplace and Marketplace Center, which are both contiguous, and the changes encourage visitor use between these two Boston landmarks.

The area around 20 and 21 Custom House Street is part of the Custom House National Historic District. Recent renovations have created an enjoyable pedestrian streetscape and transformed the area into a setting for large gatherings, festival celebrations, and the like. The architects accomplished this through the construction of two mixed-use buildings, the reconstruction of four local streets, and innovative streetscape improvements. The construction was done with an eye to maintaining harmony with neighboring buildings.

20-21 Custom House Street (3)
John Copley and Associates

Boston's 8.8-acre City Hall Plaza was created as part of the 60-acre Government Center urban renewal project in the early 1960s. The first proposals for the project—by such prominent architects and planners as Kevin Lynch and I. M. Pei—suggested the creation of a large civic space which would become the center of new city, state, and federal offices and thereby rejuvenate the core of the city. The winners of the 1962 competition to design the new city hall and its plaza, Kallmann, McKinnell, and Knowles created a powerful expressionist form, symbolizing the authority and organization of city government. The building's lower levels were originally intended to contain a beer garden with seating spilling out onto the plaza, but this was never realized.

Boston City Hall Plaza (4)
Government Center
Kallman, McKinnell, and Knowles; Chan Kreiger with Hargreaves Associates

A recently proposed redesign of the plaza would intensify activity at the edges and create a more habitable space at the center. Hargreaves Associates proposes to add a green space of lawn and trees and a large fountain which will give the plaza a more human scale yet still allow space for the large political rallies, urban festivals, farmer's markets, and sporting events that traditionally happen here.

5. The Holocaust Memorial

Carmen Park between
Union and Congress Streets

Stanley Saitowitz

The Holocaust Memorial near Government Center is a deeply symbolic structure comprising six glass towers reminiscent of chimneys or memorial candles. Six million numbers etched on these towers represent the six million Jews who perished in the Holocaust. The numbers cast shadows that fall on visitors. Under the towers, steel grates release steam that represents both smoke from the crematoriums and the warm breath of the victims. The towers stand at a height between that of the tall buildings of the financial district and the low buildings of Quincy Market. The park's location on the Freedom Trail provokes thoughts on the nature of freedom.

6. Mayor James Michael Curley Memorial Park

North and Congress Street

Carol R. Johnson Associates

This small park transformed a formerly unused median strip into much needed open space within a congested area in downtown Boston. It commemorates one of Boston's most colorful mayors with two bronze statues and serves as a focal point for the neighborhood. The simple but elegant design consists of a circular paved space with benches from which to view the statuary, all surrounded by pear trees, a lawn, and a yew hedge.

7. Waterfront Park/ Columbus Park

Atlantic Avenue

Sasaki Associates;
Shirley Muirhead;
Walker-Kluesing Design Group

Directly on the waterfront, this six-acre park is the last link in the *Walk to the Sea*, a continuous chain of open spaces from Government Center to the harbor via the historic Faneuil Hall/Quincy Market district. Highlighting the magnificent view, sloped lawns and seating walls face the harbor, while an enormous barrel-vaulted wisteria-covered wooden trellis shades the area. It also features a rose garden honoring Rose Fitzgerald Kennedy, designed by Shirley Muirhead of the Boston Redevelopment Authority, and several children's play areas. As conceived by the designers, both tourists and nearby residents can enjoy the park. The project received a BSLA Merit Award for Mature Projects in 1986.

Visitors to Columbus Park, formerly known as Waterfront Park, can see the Massachusetts Beirut Memorial that honors nine Massachusetts Marines killed in a terrorist attack in Beirut, Lebanon. Created by Walker-Kluesing Design Group, the memorial takes the form of a circle, symbolic of unity and infinity, cut into an embankment and framed by a larger circle of nine Kousa Dogwoods.

8. Long Wharf

Atlantic Avenue

Sasaki Associates

Once an active wharf, this area had deteriorated significantly by the 1980s, becoming both an eyesore and a hazard. Following historical research and community input, the designers reenvisioned the wharf as a park that would provide an acre of open space for downtown Boston. The park features a lower perimeter walk for tour and commuter boats and an upper promenade with harbor views. A compass rose on the promenade educates interested visitors, displaying information on navigation in the harbor. This project received a BSLA Merit Award for Urban Design in 1990.

9. Harbor Towers

India Wharf

The Architects Collaborative

During the redevelopment of these twin forty-story apartment buildings into condominiums, the surrounding barren and treeless landscape was also transformed. The area is now connected to the waterfront, so the landscape design had to incorporate hardy plant species such as wild roses and juniper that can resist salt spray and winds. Realignment of the entry drive provides covered drop-offs and visitor parking, and other site improvements include lighting, outdoor furniture, and signage. In 1986 this project received a BSLA Merit Award for Multi-Family Housing. More recently, the waterfront area around Harbor Towers together with a new addition to the Boston Aquarium have integrated the plaza with the new harbor-front landscape.

King's Chapel and the Granary are two of sixteen historic burial grounds within Boston which honor community founders, Revolutionary War heroes, and outstanding historic figures. These two cemeteries are also outdoor museums and urban open spaces, and as such require protection and preservation. Master plans for these burial grounds, first by Pressley Associates and later updated and expanded by Walker-Kluesing, include both general and specific recommendations for maintenance and management that will ensure that these aspects of our cultural heritage will be preserved for future generations.

King's Chapel and the Granary Cemeteries (10)
Tremont Street

Pressley Associates;
Walker-Kluesing Design Group

This 1.7-acre park sits in the heart of downtown Boston's financial district. Formerly a four-story parking garage, the site now contains a seven-floor underground parking facility with a surface-level park. In the park are over 125 species of plants; some of them are mature specimens on a unique, long-term loan from the Arnold Arboretum. Plazas at either end of the park exhibit fountains and sculpture. A restaurant, newsstand, and flower stall attract office workers and tourists to this inviting space. This project won a BSLA Award for Park and Recreational Facilities Design in 1992 and an ASLA Award and numerous other awards in 1993.

Post Office Square Park (11)
Congress, Milk, Pearl,
and Water Streets

The Halvorson Company

This 1912 park memorializes George Thorndike Angell, the founder of an early animal cruelty prevention society. The park's fountain, originally designed to provide water to horses, has been renovated twice: in 1957 garden space was added around the fountain, and in 1982 a Creature Pond was built. The pond contains bronze sculptures of lily pads and animals and is encircled with a granite ring inscribed with a quote from Angell. The revitalized park creates a tranquil and safe place in the middle of a dense urban environment. It received a BSLA Award of Excellence in 1986.

Angell Memorial Park (12)
Congress and Pearl Streets

Earl R. Flansburgh and Associates;
City-Life Boston; Shirley Muirhead

This heavily used park in the Downtown Crossing shopping area provides a resting place for shoppers and workers, as well as entry to the MBTA subway. In the park stands a honey locust tree dedicated to Boston by its sister city of Kyoto, Japan. The subway headhouse features a geometrical entrance designed in collaboration with artist Siah Armejani; it has a brick and granite base with tiered steps that provide seating. Skylights fitted with stained glass panels are set within the structure to allow light to filter below ground into the subway. In 1990 this project received a BSLA Merit Award for Urban Design.

(13) Shopper's Park
Downtown Crossing MBTA Station

Childs, Bertman, Tseckares, and Casendino (CBT)

Winthrop Lane, which connects the Downtown Crossing shopping district to the financial district, was transformed by CBT from a rundown alley to a pleasant pedestrian walkway with brick paving, greenhouse additions for retail use, and period lighting. Included in the alley pavement are one hundred bronze bricks depicting life in Boston, both past and present. Known as "Boston Bricks," these bronze reliefs are the creation of local artists Kate Burke and Gregg LeFevre.

(14) Winthrop Lane
Childs, Bertman, Tseckares, and Casendino (CBT)

This small park located within one of the busiest commercial districts of the city, was renovated in 1995. Its brick pavers with granite accent banding help to integrate the park into its historical surroundings. Mature trees, shrubs, colorful perennials, and groundcovers offer a pleasant contrast to the surrounding urban environment. The former home of the Boston Record American Newspaper, this project is an early example of adaptive re-use architecture, and CBT's work on it helped to earn the firm a Special Award from The National Trust for Historic Preservation.

(15) One Winthrop Square
Corner of Devonshire and Otis Streets

The Halvorson Company; Childs, Bertman, Tseckares, and Casendino (CBT)

(16) Irish Famine Memorial
Washington Street at School Street

Casendino and Company, with Cecil and Rizvi

This small downtown park was built in memory of the Irish Famine, honoring the 150th anniversary of the end of the famine in 1847. The design features an enclosed contemplative space along with an open public space in this busy downtown location. Sculptor Robert Shure created two works for the memorial: one depicting a family leaving Ireland destitute and poor, the other a family arriving in Boston filled with hope and determination.

(17) Downtown Crossing
Washington Street

Wallace Floyd Associates

This project helped to revitalize the pedestrian and retail environment of Boston's Washington Street shopping district, known as Downtown Crossing. Improvements included the reconstruction of a pedestrian mall as well as the introduction of new street lighting, seating, and plantings. Designers developed a set of façade and awning guidelines for the area's historic buildings that preserve the architectural integrity of the neighborhood and contribute to its visual appeal.

Paving details, seating, and street plantings enhance the pedestrian environment around this building. The design also successfully relates and extends the distinctive urban landscape of the Post Office Square Park located across the street.

New England Telephone Headquarters
185 Franklin Street
The Halvorson Company

This third-floor roof garden features a variety of comfortable sitting areas and mature plantings. These plantings—hardy, formally pruned evergreens—have survived two decades of high winds. The sitting areas, enclosed with curved seating benches, are bordered with beds of beach stone and river-washed pea stone, raked in the Japanese style. The garden received a BSLA Merit Award for Commercial Design.

Federal Reserve Bank of Boston, Roof Garden
600 Atlantic Avenue
Hugh Stubbins Associates

The Central Artery/Tunnel Project is the largest civil engineering project in the United States. Three new tunnels are under construction beneath both the city itself and Boston Harbor that will carry highway traffic through Boston (replacing the elevated Central Artery) and link downtown Boston to Logan Airport. The completed project, currently estimated to cost $11 billion, will consist of over 161 lane-miles of highway in a 7.5 mile corridor and accommodate 245,000 vehicles per day. Over 13 million cubic yards of earth will be excavated, and four major interchanges plus several minor connections will be built. The entire existing highway system, which currently carries over 190,000 vehicles per day, and the city streets beneath and around the new system will remain fully operational during the entire eleven-year construction period.

Central Artery/ Third Harbor Tunnel
Interstate 93
Carol R. Johnson Associates;
Copley/Wolff Joint Venture;
The Cecil Group; Brown and
Rowe; HNTB; Paul Lu Associates;
Pressley Associates;
Sasaki Associates

The project will create more than 150 acres of new parks and open space: 27 acres downtown where the existing artery will be demolished; 105 acres on Spectacle Island, which has been filled and capped using excavated material from the project; 33 acres in the lower basin of the Charles River, which will be an extension of the Esplanade; and 7 acres in East Boston.

Preliminary design for the surface restoration of the Central Artery/Ted Williams Tunnel project was developed by Carol R. Johnson Associates, who prepared the project-wide design guidelines and landscape design details for each section of the new artery. Final design for the surface restoration of the downtown Boston area from Congress Street to Causeway Street was completed by Copley/Wolff Joint Venture. This group produced final streetscape design, detailing structural soils, planting design, and implemented art projects. Final designs for remaining sections are being prepared by The Cecil Group; Brown and Rowe; HNTB; Paul Lu Associates; Pressley Associates; and Sasaki Associates, with CRJA, who is providing ongoing project coordination.

This park, beside the gateway with its ceremonial white lion guards, welcomes people to Chinatown. A red "Chinese Chippendale" wrought-iron fence encloses and defines the park. Inside, there is play equipment for children and comfortable purpleheart timber benches for resting. Honey locust trees shade the hand-tight brickwork pavement pattern. Light fixtures throughout follow the Chinatown standard. In 1985 this project received a BSLA Merit Award for Park Design.

Chinatown Gateway Park
Corner of Hudson and Beach
Streets, Chinatown, Boston
Shirley M. Muirhead

*N*orth End

Located in Boston's North End along the Freedom Trail, this pedestrian mall links the Old North Church to Hanover Street and provides important open space in this dense urban environment. Recent renovation has restored the central fountain and added illumination, constructed new seating and stone planters, and reconstructed wrought-iron gates, bollards, and chains at the street edge.

Copp's Hill Terrace in Boston's oldest neighborhood, the North End, was designed in 1894 by Charles Eliot, founder of the Metropolitan Park System, and was recently named to the National Register of Historic Places. Copp's Hill was Boston's original waterfront park, offering views to Charlestown from its upper terrace. Recent improvements by Wallace Floyd include the restoration of the park's granite block walls and steps, tree planting, and new compatible furnishings. A dilapidated shelter was removed and replaced with trees and seating in keeping with Eliot's original intent.

*B*eacon Hill

A 1990 restoration of the Massachusetts State House included replacing an existing parking lot with a three-level underground parking garage covered over by a rooftop garden. This formal promenade-style garden is reminiscent of the earlier East Park which occupied the site one hundred years ago. The garden features formal arrangements of decorative flower beds, shrub borders, and lawn panels.

Perhaps the most famous of Boston's residential parks, Louisburg Square was the first privately owned and managed urban space in the United States. This beautiful square, in the middle of historic Beacon Hill, is bordered by many architecturally and historically significant buildings. The square was designed on the model of eighteenth- and early nineteenth-century London squares. It is surrounded by a lovely iron fence.

Back Bay - Charles River

Copley Square—named for John Singleton Copley, a prominent painter of the late eighteenth century—became a park in 1883 as part of the Back Bay landfill and development project. Strategically located at the joining of the grids of Back Bay and the South End, the 2.4-acre square is defined by some of Boston's most prominent architecture: H.H. Richardson's Trinity Church, McKim Mead and White's Public Library with its Philip Johnson addition, and I.M. Pei's Hancock Tower.

In the twentieth century the park was compromised by the addition of new roads and trolley lines, the demolition of several key architectural and cultural features, and urban renewal efforts. In 1965 an international competition was held to redesign the park. Sasaki Associates won, and the renovations were completed in 1969. The Sasaki plan sunk the plaza below street level to highlight the buildings and to allow park users to get away from the sight, sound, and smell of the traffic. Low concrete walls were added around the square to further screen automobiles from view. The Sasaki plan attempted a grand gesture: a European-type urban plaza that would enhance the stature of the surrounding buildings.

The park had deteriorated by the 1980s, however, so in 1984 another design competition was sponsored by the National Endowment for the Arts and the Boston Redevelopment Authority. The design jury, chaired by William H. Whyte, noted expert on public use of urban space, chose a design by Dean Abbott of Clarke and Raupano. This redesign was completed in 1989. It creates a "living room" for the neighborhood and a "front yard" for the Trinity Church and the Boston Public Library. The design is an abstraction of the New England village green and includes a major multipurpose fountain that serves as a performance space when the water is gone. Abbott's design recalls the pre-Sasaki park that was bisected diagonally by Huntington Avenue.

Copley Square (26)

Boylston and Dartmouth Streets, Back Bay

Sasaki Associates; Clarke and Raupano

The Boston Marathon Centennial Monument, by Mark C. Flannery, was added to Copley Square in 1996 to celebrate the one-hundredth running of the Boston Marathon. Constructed of multicolored granite, it represents the diverse group of people who participate in the race. The monument received a BSLA Merit Award for Landscape, Art, and Earth Sculpture.

Boston Marathon Monument (27)

Copley Square, Boylston and Dartmouth Streets, Back Bay

Mark C. Flannery

(28) Boston Public Library Courtyard

Copley Square

Frederick Law Olmsted Sr.;
Walker-Kluesing Design Group

The Boston Public Library is housed in a national historic landmark, the 1895 McKim, Mead, and White renaissance revival structure with a 1972 addition by Philip Johnson. The interior courtyard design was inspired by the Cancelleria in Rome, bringing light into the center of the building and providing a tranquil outdoor space. The courtyard's landscape design engaged a number of Boston firms including the Olmsted firm and the Manning Brothers. A current rehabilitation by Walker-Kluesing will return the Bacchante sculpture to the courtyard; it has been absent since Puritanical voices demanded its removal in 1896. The historic Dartmouth Street main entrance was recently reopened and an expanded pedestrian area will soon create a stronger link between the library and Copley Square.

(29) The New England Life Insurance Building

501 Boylston Street

The Halvorson Company

The addition of street-level retail shops and various streetscape improvements form the core of this project. Granite planters with historic detailing hold evergreen and flowering plants. Subtle color changes in the paving delineate public and private sidewalk zones and clarify pedestrian circulation. The Halvorson Company also prepared a streetscape master plan for the City of Boston to establish visual unity and coherence along the length of Boylston Street.

(30) Church Court Condominiums

490 Beacon Street at
Harvard Bridge

Carol R. Johnson Associates

Church Court Condominiums is good example of adaptive reuse. This former church, located within the historic Back Bay neighborhood, now houses luxury condominium units. A pleasant courtyard garden covers the roof deck of an underground garage, sensitively integrating the garage with its historic surroundings.

Located in Boston's historic Back Bay, the Clarendon Street Playground serves as the neighborhood playground. Originally developed in the late ninteen-sixties on the site of two demolished row houses, the park retains the outline of the bowed fronts of both houses. The significant magnolia and sycamore trees, planted when the park was first established, have been preserved during its recent renovation. CBA Landscape Architects re-designed the park to provide more play opportunities for children and more amenities for adults. Organized around a raised central area planted with flowering pear trees, the park offers the visitor three areas of play equipment, an open area for games, a large sand box and gathering area, benches, sitting walls, storage shed, water fountain, and bulletin board.

Clarendon Street Playground (31)

Clarendon Street and Commonwealth Avenue, Back Bay

CBA Landscape Architects

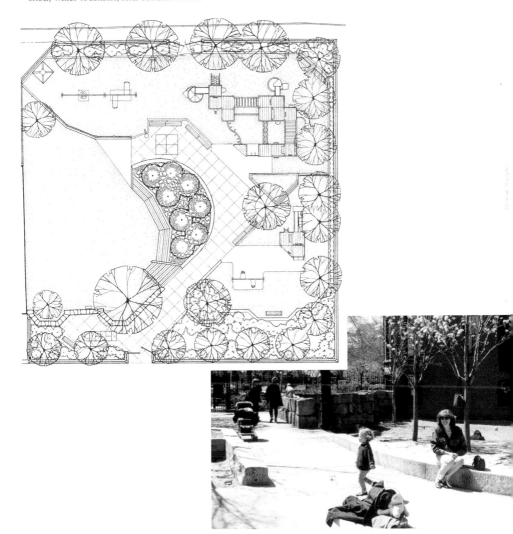

Copley Place, a grand in-town shopping mall, contains interior landscapes which integrate the inside and outside design of the development. Materials around the exterior of doorways carry through into the building. Similar color choices and surface treatment of materials throughout the central atrium, retail spaces, and exterior areas help to unify the entire project. Major sculptural work and a dominant water feature attract the interest of shoppers.

Copley Place, Interior (32)

The Architects Collaborative

(33) New Charles River Basin

Charles River between the
Charles River Esplanade
and Boston Harbor,
Cambridge and Boston

Carr, Lynch, Hack, and Sandell
with Oehme van Sweden and
Associates; The Halvorson
Company; Pressley Associates;
Carol R. Johnson Associates

The New Charles River Basin is a major effort in environmental restoration and design associated with the Central Artery/Third Harbor Tunnel project. The project will restore the mouth of the Charles River, transforming it from an inaccessible urban river wasteland into a model urban greenway with over forty acres of parks and riverfront walks, linking the Charles River Basin Esplanade with Boston Harbor for the first time. The master plan developed by Carr, Lynch, Hack, and Sandell includes five new parks: North Point Meadows (Carr Lynch), Nashua Street Park (The Halvorson Company), Revere Landing Park (Carr Lynch), the historic North and South Dam (Pressley Associates), and Lovejoy Wharf (Childs Engineering with Carol R. Johnson Associates). Gateways will link the parks and walkways with adjacent communities.

As part of the Charles River Reservation and the larger Metropolitan Park System, interpretive presentations developed for the New Basin will explore the river's ecological system and the stewardship of the Metropolitan District Commission (MDC). By expanding on the theme of connections, the master plan will consider the relationship between the city and the river and the evolution of Boston's built environment. Proposed new pedestrian walks will connect the Cambridge and Boston riverfronts.

The basin project, managed by the MDC and Bechtel/Parsons Joint Venture, started construction in 1995 with Revere Landing Park, now complete. The remaining parks and walkways are scheduled for construction after the Central Artery is completed early in the next century.

(34) Charles River Basin Esplanade

Storrow Drive

Arthur A. Shurcliff

The first phase of this recreational project involved improvement of the shores along the Charles River, including widening the shore, planting several varieties of trees, the design of the Music Oval, and a lagoon for safe boating and ice skating. Ten years later, the second phase involved the integration of Storrow Drive into this strip of land between the River and existing older neighborhoods. It included the reconstruction of several recreational features lost to the highway, two new lagoons, and a pedestrian overpass, named for the Boston Pops Orchestra's legendary conductor Arthur Fiedler, at the Hatch Music Shell.

Though planned in 1801 by the great Boston architect Charles Bulfinch, these two parks were not constructed until the 1860s. Square in shape, they sit across from each other along Washington Street. The parks are identical in layout, consisting of diagonal paths with a fountain located at the intersection. This highly symmetrical design creates a formal, grand space unlike other open spaces in the South End which are generally more informal in style.

Blackstone and Franklin Squares ㉟

Washington Street at West Newton Street

Charles Bulfinch

The unique fluted shape of this South End park arises from rows of bowfront houses, which create a pleasing rhythm in their repetition. All of the houses have high front stairs which place the main entry on the second floor, creating what is called an English basement on the first. The park contains grass and mature trees enclosed by iron fencing, features which soften the urban environment and provide the residents of this neighborhood with open space for outdoor activity.

Worcester Square ㊱

Worcester Street between Washington and Harrison Streets

Renovated by Patrice Todisco and Roger B. Erickson

This oval park is surrounded by three and four story brick bowfront houses with dormered upper floor windows and high front stairs (which originally had elaborate cast-iron balustrades). Its narrow form is based upon English urban planning principles and possibly the influence of Charles Bulfinch. The square predates the Back Bay, which was developed around boulevards and green spaces in the French style.

Concord Square ㊲

Between Tremont Street and Columbus Avenue

This lovely square was one of the first of the South End parks to be completed. The surrounding Victorian brick row houses step forward at the ends of the square, creating an oval shape and a pleasing sense of enclosure. Much of the ornamental ironwork is noteworthy, including some fine Victorian cast-iron fencing. The park contains two fountains, flower plantings, and mature trees, softening the urban environment and providing residents with open space for recreation.

Union Park ㊳

Between Tremont Street and Shawmut Avenue ▼

This narrow park, planted with trees and grass and enclosed by an iron fence, runs through the center portion of one city block. Despite its small size it provides a focal point and identity for the block, contributing far more in this manner than would a roadway. The facing Italianate bowfront houses and the thin band of green space are a modest version of larger and more elaborate South End squares.

Rutland Square ㊴

Between Tremont Street and Columbus Avenue

This block of former retail shops and houses became vacant after a thwarted highway project in the 1960s and was later appropriated for farming by nearby Chinese families. Their efforts to improve this rubbled block with night soil and found materials were soon met with guidance and support from a city program. Within the garden, rows of tall wooden posts mark a communal walkway while personal touches like lattice and fencing make each plot the gardener's own. This garden space, now a protected use, shows the adaptation of traditional Chinese horticultural practices to a new environment in Boston's South End. The garden reflects the changing face of this neighborhood.

Berkeley Street Community Garden ㊵

Berkeley Street extending from Tremont Street to Shawmut Avenue

South End/Lower Roxbury Open Space Land Trust; Berkeley Street Community Gardeners; Ralph Fan Yee; Michael Immel; Stephanie Bothwell; Julie Stone; and Paul C. K. Lu

(41) James Hayes Park

West Canton Street and
Warren Avenue

Ann G. Johnson Associates

There had been a neighborhood park on this South End site for eighteen years until subsurface settling made the area unsafe. To correct the problem, designers developed an extensive geotextile-reinforced underdrain system. The new design has a simple circular pattern that accommodates long-established diagonal pedestrian paths though the site. Materials in the park blend with those of the surrounding neighborhood, and plantings provide year-round interest. This project received a BSLA Merit Award in 1992, an Urban Landscape Award in 1993, and a Preservation Award in 1993.

(42) Tent City

▼ 130 Dartmouth Street,

The Halvorson Company

Dedicated in 1988, Tent City is one of Boston's largest mixed-income housing developments. It spans an entire city block and includes several apartment buildings, duplexes, and an underground parking lot. Corridors link the buildings to each other, creating a pleasant residential environment with quality outdoor spaces. One significant achievement of this urban design is its connection to three key areas of the city: the Copley Square commercial area, the Southwest Corridor subway station and linear park, and the South End residential neighborhood.

Located on the heavily traveled Columbus Avenue, Harriet Tubman Park is a visual and cultural landmark in Boston's South End. Rebuilt in 1999, it was redesigned to display two significant bronze sculptures. One contemporary sculpture, by Fern Cunningham, honors Harriet Tubman, a leading abolitionist and "conductor" of the Underground Railway. The other sculpture, by Meta Warrick Fuller, was sculpted in 1913 (but not cast until 1999) to commemorate the fiftieth anniversary of the Emancipation Proclamation. The park also has bronze plaques made by middle school children that depict the life of Ms. Tubman. The park is enclosed by an ornamental iron fence, designed by the landscape architect to complement the spirit of the sculpture.

(43) Harriet Tubman Park

Columbus Avenue and
Pembroke Street, South End

CBA Landscape Architects

_H_untington Avenue – Fenway

The Garden Court was established when the decorative arts wing was added to the museum in 1928, creating a large enclosed courtyard space. Arthur A. Shurcliff prepared the design featuring a central octagonal fountain and a paved upper terrace bounded by a balustrade and stairs that lead to the lower garden level. Symmetrical paths enclose grassy areas, and space is provided for sculpture and plantings. After construction of the new museum wing in 1983, the garden was closed to the public. The restoration, by Pressley Associates in 1995, used historic photographic documentation to accurately restore Shurcliff's original design.

In 1989, the museum created a Japanese walled garden, "Tenshin-en, The Heart of Heaven." Designed by noted Japanese "garden master," Kinsaku Nakane, in collaboration with the Halvorson Company and Messervy Associates, it is a karesansui or dry landscape that includes the horai elements of mountains, stones, and islands, symbols of hope, longevity, and immortality "Tenshin-en" can be seen from a granite viewing terrace within the garden or from the second floor of the museum. It is New England's only semipublic viewing garden of this style. Because museum pieces are set within the garden, it also functions as an outdoor exhibit gallery. The garden received a BSLA Merit Award for Landscape Art in 1990.

> ### Boston Museum of Fine Arts, Italian Garden Court and Japanese Garden (44)
>
> Huntington Avenue
>
> Arthur A. Shurcliff; Pressley Associates; Nakane Garden Research; Messervy Associates, and The Halvorson Company

The former home of wealthy socialite and art collector Isabella Stewart Gardener is now a world-renowned art museum featuring her wonderful, wide-ranging collection. The highlight of the building is a large Renaissance-style enclosed courtyard garden which rises four stories to multi-paned glass skylights above. From the cloisters on ground level to the balconies and windows of Venetian design above, the courtyard is graced with many different vantage points from which to view the garden. Throughout the year the garden features lush flower displays that change monthly.

> ### Isabella Stewart Gardener Museum – Courtyard (45)
>
> 280 The Fenway
>
> Isabella Stewart Gardner

Northeastern University's grounds were previously cold, hard, drab, and uninviting. Over a hundred improvements to quadrangles, linkage spaces, peripheral areas, and gateways have reshaped the campus and unified it. Pedestrian malls, for example, now tie the Main Quadrangle to other parts of campus such as the Library Quadrangle. The university's Bulfinch Mall and the Sculpture Park are both linkage spaces connecting major campus quadrangles as well as comfortable open spaces for contemplative activities. In 1990 the Library Quadrangle received a BSLA Honor Award for Institutional Design, and in 1992 this work was honored at the White House with a National Landscape Award.

Headquarters of the First Church of Christ Scientist, the Christian Science Center was an urban renewal project which consolidated various functions of the Church's worldwide activities. The center includes the mother church, several newer buildings designed by architect I. M. Pei, and nine acres of open space. The dominant unifying element is a monumental 675-foot-long reflecting pool that ends in a round fountain with radiating jets. The new site design preserved many existing plants, including twenty-seven mature American lindens. The project received ASLA and BSLA Honor Awards in 1987 and 1988, respectively.

First laid out by Frederick Law Olmsted in his 1879 master plan for the Back Bay Fens, this entrance gate to the park was designed in 1901 by Guy Lowell. It is a fine example of the Victorian style and reflects the urban aristocratic pride of the Back Bay. Restoration work included replacing missing sculpture and balustrades, repointing and cleaning those still standing, and installing new plantings and paving. This project contributes significantly to the architectural and landscape preservation efforts in the historic Back Bay neighborhood.

Map 2 – Boston, Brookline, Cambridge

The Emerald Necklace
49. Emerald Necklace, Master Plan
50. Boston Common
51. Boston Public Garden
52. Commonwealth Avenue Mall
53. Back Bay Fens
54. The Riverway and Olmsted Park
55. Jamaica Pond
56. The Arnold Arboretum of Harvard University
57. Franklin Park

Charlestown
58. City Square Park
59. Shipyard Park
60. Shipyard Park, Phase III
61. Shipyard Quarters
62. Doherty Playground
63. Warren Prescott Schoolyard

East Boston
64. East Boston Piers Park
65. The Harborwalk at
    Logan International Airport
66. Logan Airport Hilton
67. Hugh Roe O'Donnell Schoolyard
68. Eagle Hill Memorial Community Garden

South Boston/ Harborfront
69. The Harborwalk
70. United States Federal Court House
71. World Trade Center/
    Seaport Hotel/Northern Avenue
72. Pier 10 Park
73. Cella Park and Harborwalk
74. Castle Island Playground
75. South Boston Beaches Restoration

Roxbury
76. Southwest Corridor Park
77. Roxbury Heritage State Park
78. Dudley Town Common
79. Holborn Street Totlot Renovation
80. Ruggles Plaza and Streetscape
81. Orchard Park Housing Development
82. Grant Manor Housing

Dorchester
83. JFK Library
84. Harbor Point Housing
85. Old Harbor Park
86. Dorchester Heights Monument and
    Thomas Park

Jamaica Plain
87. Temple Israel
88. Forbes Street Community Garden
89. Forest Hills
90. Mozart Park

Brookline
91. Larz Anderson Park
92. Fairsted
93. Corey Hill Park

Longwood Area
94. Harvard Medical School Main Quadrangle
95. Longwood Medical Research Center
96. The Clinical Center, Beth Israel Hospital
97. New England Baptist Hospital Courtyards
98. The Children's Hospital Gateway Park and
    Winter Garden
99. New England Deaconess Hospital
100. Myles Elliott and Eugenia Louise Sweeney
    Field

Allston – Brighton
101. Gardner Street Park
102. Commonwealth Development
103. Genzyme Corporation
104. Gallatin Hall, Harvard Business School
105. Chase Hall, Harvard Business School

CAMBRIDGE
Harvard Square
106. Harvard Square
107. Winthrop Park
108. John Fitzgerald Kennedy Memorial Park
109. Charles Square
110. Quincy Square
111. Longfellow National Historic Site
112. University Green

Harvard University
113. Harvard Yard - Master Plan
114. Tanner Fountain
115. Quincy House
116. Harvard Univ. DeWolfe Street Housing
117. Harvard Law School

MIT - Kendall Square
118. Massachusetts Institute of Technology
    McDermott Court
119. University Park at M.I.T.
120. Cambridge Center/Kendall Square
121. Cambridge Center North Park,
    Kendall Square
122. Cambridge Center Garage Roof Garden
123. Biogen, Inc.
124. Newtowne Court

East Cambridge
125. Lechmere Canal Park
126. Charles Park
127. Centanni Way
128. Bulfinch Courthouse Square

Cambridge/Watertown
129. Mount Auburn Cemetery
130. Buckingham, Browne & Nichols School,
    Athletic Facility

Winter on the Boston Common

Fresh
Pond

Brattle St.

Harvard
Square

Kirkland St.

111

112

Mount Auburn St.

Hampshire St.

Cambridge St.

114
117
113

109

106

110

Broadway

12

East
Cambridg

128

129

130

Mt. Auburn
Cemetery

108

107

116

115

Massachusetts Ave.

120

121

122

123

Soldiers
Field

Soldiers Field Rd.

104

105

Western

Ave.

Cambridge

Main St.

Kendall
Square

124

Greenough Blvd

Coolidge Ave.

Franklin St.

Allston

103

90

Magazine St.

Sidney St.

119

118

MIT

Paul Dudley White Bike Pa

Brighton Ave.

Charles River

Back Bay

Ave.

Commonwealth

Commonwealth

Harvard St.

93

St.

Longwood Ave.

Back Bay
Fens

53

102

Beacon

St.

99

98

95

Huntington Ave.

100

96

94

80

82

76

Brooklin
Reservoir

97

54

Brookline

Columbus Ave.

Roxbury

St.

77

92

Warren

87

Washington

Warren St.

Cottage

49

Perkins St

Lee St.

Ave.

88

90

Clyde

Goddard

Larz
Anderson
Park

Jamaica Pond

55

Humboldt Ave

79

Country
Club

91

Newton St.

Pond St.

Jamaica
Plain

Green St.

76

Glen Rd.

57

Carolina

Walnut
Hill Cemetery

Arborway

Williams

Circuit

Franklin
Park

56

VFW Parkway

101

Arnold
Arboretum

Morton

Blue Hill Ave

Talbot Ave

Forest Hills
Cemetery

89

Franklin
Field

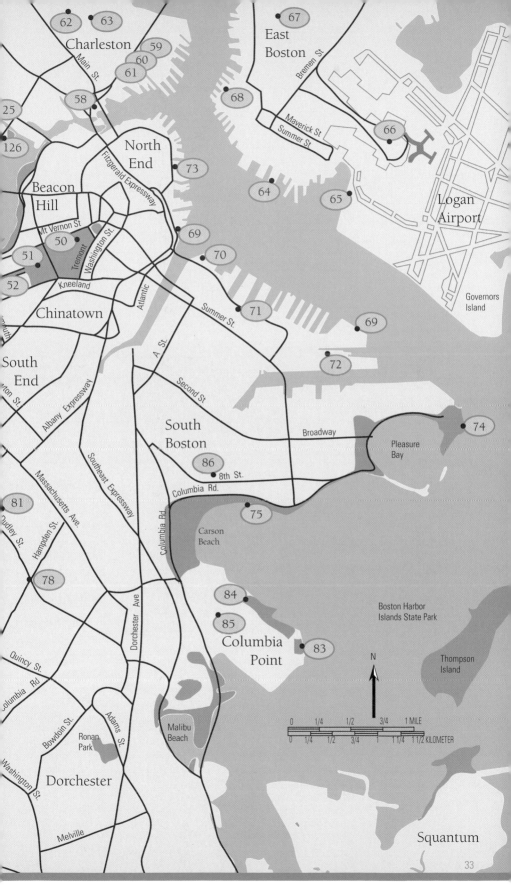

Charleston

62 63

59

60

61

58

25

126

North
End

73

Beacon
Hill

Mt Vernon St

50

Tremont

51

Washington St.

52

Kneeland

Chinatown

South
End

Albany Expressway

Southeast Expressway

81

Dudley St.

78

Hampden St.

Massachusetts Ave.

Quincy St.

Columbia Rd.

Bowdoin St.

Washington St.

Ronan
Park

Adams St.

Dorchester

Melville

Dorchester Ave

Columbia Rd.

Malibu
Beach

Columbia
Point

84

85

83

East
Boston

67

Bremen St.

68

Maverick St

Summer St

64

Logan
Airport

66

65

Governors
Island

69

70

Summer St.

A St.

Second St

71

69

72

Broadway

Pleasure
Bay

74

South
Boston

86

8th St.

Columbia Rd.

75

Carson
Beach

Boston Harbor
Islands State Park

Thompson
Island

N

Squantum

0   1/4   1/2   3/4   1 MILE

0   1/4   1/2   3/4   1   1 1/4   1 1/2 KILOMETER

33

The Emerald Necklace

(49) Emerald Necklace, Master Plan

Boston and Brookline

Massachusetts Department of Environmental Management; Pressley Associates; Walmsley /Pressley Joint Venture

This exciting project, begun in 1985 and coordinated by the Olmsted Historic Preservation Program of the Massachusetts Department of Environmental Management, includes the restoration of four of Olmsted's Emerald Necklace parks: the Back Bay Fens, the Riverway, Olmsted Park, and Jamaica Pond. Comprising five hundred acres of parkland and watercourse, these parks stretch through varied terrain and neighborhoods in a linear fashion. The master plan is attempting to overcome the physical and aesthetic barriers that impact the parks today; it seeks to reestablish the forms created by Olmsted; and it sets forth a maintenance and management plan. Since 1985, original stone bridges have been repaired, landscape elements have been reconstructed, Victory Gardens have been rehabilitated, and bicycle and pedestrian pathways have been constructed.

(50) Boston Common

Beacon, Boylston, Charles, Park, and Tremont Streets, Boston

Brown and Rowe; Carol R. Johnson and Associates; Lynn Wolff Associates; John Copley and Associates; Walker-Kluesing Design Group

Boston Common is the oldest public open space in the United States, dating to the early seventeenth century, well before the establishment of the profession of landscape architecture in America. For over 375 years the Boston Common has been a green oasis in the expanding city and a mirror reflecting the broad range of events unfolding in Boston and the nation. Today the Common is the eastern "jewel" in the Emerald Necklace (Boston's famous connected park and parkway network), providing 50 acres of wooded groves and open lawn areas.

In 1974 a master plan for the Common, prepared by Carol R. Johnson and Associates, solved long-term circulation problems by adding the "mayor's walk," a new east-west route leading to the Statehouse. In 1991 the Walker Kluesing Design Group prepared another master plan: this one identifies significant attributes of the common to be preserved, and it sets policies for maintenance and administration. This master plan received a BSLA Merit Award for Landscape Planning in 1991 and an ASLA Merit Award for Communication in 1992.

Lynn Wolff Associates and John Copley and Associates recently renovated the historic Frog Pond so that it can be enjoyed during all four seasons. In the spring and fall it is a reflecting pool featuring a historic plume fountain. During the summer it becomes a wading pool with a spray for children, and during the winter it operates as an ice skating rink. The complex mechanical equipment needed for these various functions is buried underground so that it does not mar the site's historic character. This adaptive reuse project received the 1997 Preservation Achievement Award from the Boston Preservation Alliance, an Urban Landscape Award from the Massachusetts Horticultural Society, and an award for Parks and Recreational Design from the BSLA.

As part of recent renovations, the Boston Common Visitor Center was moved to a more prominent location. Brown and Rowe sited the building so that it fit into the historic landscape of the Common. New grass and deciduous trees are in keeping with the Common's historic New England simplicity.

Originally called the Boston Botanical Gardens, the Public Garden is a quintessential Victorian park. Built entirely on landfill, it was first used by amateur horticulturists for greenhouses containing imported rare plants. In the 1850s the city acquired the property, and George Meacham, a local architect, laid out plans for a garden which combined picturesque and formal elements. It includes an irregularly shaped pond and curving pathways, as well as a strong axial connection to Commonwealth Avenue, geometrical flower beds, and a statue of George Washington. Its development served to spur even more ambitious park programs including Charles Eliot's Metropolitan Park System. The park is beloved by Boston's children for its swan boats and bronzed "Make Way for Ducklings" sculpture. A master plan for the Public Gardens was prepared by Carol R. Johnson Associates in 1974.

Commonwealth Avenue is one of the finest examples of urban planning in nineteenth-century America. Designed in the 1860s by the architect Arthur Gilman in the style of the grand French boulevard, Commonwealth Avenue is the central axis of Gilman's Back Bay. The tree-lined avenue and wide center mall of green space unify the stunning collection of Victorian homes and the many monuments and memorials within the mall. In the 1880s Frederick Law Olmsted Sr. extended the avenue, linking the Public Garden and the Boston Common with the Back Bay Fens, Brookline, and Brighton. Unfortunately Commonwealth Avenue near the Fens has been disrupted substantially in recent years through insensitive highway construction. Several blocks of the historic mall, however, have been restored by Carol Johnson Associates and Walker-Kluesing Design group. They added raised granite curbs, stonedust walks, tree plantings, and furniture.

Boston Public Garden (51)
Arlington, Beacon, Boylston, and Charles Streets, Boston
George Meacham;
Carol R. Johnson Associates

Commonwealth Avenue Mall (52)
Commonwealth Avenue, Boston
Arthur Gilman;
Carol R. Johnson Associates;
Walker-Kluesing Design Group

(53) Back Bay Fens

Boston

Frederick Law Olmsted Sr.;
Arthur A. Shurcliff;
Sidney Shurcliff;
Carol R. Johnson Associates;
Pressley Associates;
Walker-Kluesing Design Group

(Above) The Rose Garden in
Back Bay Fens

By Olmsted's time, this site had become a tidal basin that collected sewage and flooded regularly. To overcome the health and safety hazards of this area, Olmsted's design for reclamation included a buried sewage inceptor and tide gates. The reclaimed land was then sculpted into gentle, natural forms, and the water edges were planted with sedges and salt-water tolerant shrubs, creating a park that looked like a salt marsh around which the city had grown. A network of foot, carriage, and bridle pathways provided circulation throughout the park. Sadly the Fens has been much altered by the construction of highways, ramps, and memorials, so that little remains of Olmsted's original concept save the outline and a few plantings.

In the 1930's a Rose Garden designed by Sidney Shurcliff was added to the Fenway. The Fens Victory Gardens, which are still under cultivation, were begun during World War II to augment the country's war effort. Though originally used to grow vegetables, they now also grow flowers and shrubs. The long waiting list for plots attests to their popularity. Master plans for the Fens were prepared by Carol R. Johnson Associates in 1980, and by Walmsley/Pressley Joint Venture in 1989. A number of projects have been designed in the 1990's by Pressley Associates and Walker-Kluesing Design Group.

(54) The Riverway and Olmsted Park

Boston and Brookline

Frederick Law Olmsted Sr.;
Walmsley/Pressley Joint
Venture; Pressley Associates

This section of the Emerald Necklace, which Olmsted called the Muddy River Improvement, connects the Back Bay Fens to Jamaica Pond. The Muddy River became brackish and stagnant during the urbanization of the late 1800s and posed a health problem to the region. The Muddy River Improvement changed the course of the Muddy River and transformed a cattail swamp into a chain of picturesque freshwater ponds interspersed with groves of trees and meadows. A bridle path ran along one bank of the river and intersected with the Fens. The park was almost completely regraded. Because of its narrow

boundaries, its edges were planted heavily to screen out the surrounding city. Earth berms were constructed along the Brookline side of the Riverway to shield it from the sound of the railway (now the Riverside Line of the MBTA). Walmsley/Pressley Joint Venture prepared a Master Plan for the Riverway and Olmsted Park in 1989 and more recently Pressley Associates has recently designed several projects in this area.

This stretch of the Emerald Necklace contains the only large freshwater pond in the city. Unlike most of the other elements of the Emerald Necklace, Olmsted's design for this park preserved its landscape nearly unchanged, as "a natural sheet of water, with quiet graceful shores . . . shaded by a fine natural forest growth to be brought out overhangingly, darkening the water's edge and favoring great beauty in reflections and flickering half-lights" (Report of the Landscape Architect, 1881). There were already plantings of fine specimen trees around the summer homes on the park's shores, but they were all cut down. A ring path was constructed around the entire pond perimeter, and the bridle path was extended. Boating and fishing facilities were added to increase recreational opportunities for the public. Walmsley/Pressley Joint Venture prepared a Master Plan for Jamaica Pond in 1989 and more recently Pressley Associates has recently designed several restoration projects for the Pond.

Jamaica Pond (55)

Boston

Frederick Law Olmsted Sr.;
Walmsley/Pressley Joint Venture;
Pressley Associates

The design of the 265-acre world-renown Arnold Arboretum—a National Historic Landmark and a jewel of Boston's Emerald Necklace—was started 1878 by Frederick Law Olmsted Sr. and Charles Sprague Sargent, who became the Arnold's first director. The arboretum is an especially well-preserved Olmsted landscape, and the plant collection features over four thousand species of plants from all the temperate regions of the world. Today, the arboretum is a romantic landscape with curvilinear roads and rolling hills within which the plant collections are organized and displayed.

Additions and changes in the park's design have continued since it opened. In the late 1870s the Olmsted firm designed the arboretum's circulation system. Between 1883 and 1885 Charles Eliot and Henry Sargent Codman, then apprentices in the Olmsted firm, developed a series of plans for the distribution of trees in their correct botanical order. The Olmsted firm designed the Peter's Hill parcel, added in 1895, and in the 1940s, Beatrix Jones Farrand, who had studied plants at the arboretum under Charles S. Sargent, designed an azalea border along the east side of Meadow Road. Remnants of this planting can be seen today.

In 1974, the firm of Shurcliff, Merrill, and Footit redesigned the summit of Bussey Hill, adding a seating area from which visitors can take in a fine view of the Blue Hills to the south, framed by the arboretum's plantings. Sasaki Associates prepared a master plan which addressed circulation, access, and future development issues. The Linda J. Davison Rhododendron Path was designed by landscape architect Julie Messervy in 1990. This new path winds through a shaded ravine along

The Arnold Arboretum of Harvard University (56)

Arborway, Jamaica Plain
Boston

Frederick Law Olmsted Sr.;
Beatrix Jones Farrand; Shurcliff,
Merrill, and Footit; Sasaki
Associates; Julie Messervy;
Carol R. Johnson Associates

Bussey Brook and features two small waterfalls, a rustic bridge, and a stone seating area.

Carol R. Johnson Associates (CRJA) redesigned the entrance to the Hunnewell Administration Building in 1992 to comply with the Americans with Disabilities Act. A gentle earthen berm rises in front of the building to a bluestone and brick seating terrace. New plantings illustrate the botanical connections between the floras of Asia and North America. CRJA also renovated Peter's Hill in 1998, removing excessive paving and adding a new pedestrian path, plantings, and granite block seating areas.

---

(57) Franklin Park

Jamaica Plain, Boston

Frederick Law Olmsted, Sr.;
Arthur A. Shurcliff;
Massachusetts Department of
Environmental Management;
The Halvorson Company;
Johansson and Walcavage;
Pressley Associates

This five-hundred-acre park is the westernmost jewel of the Emerald Necklace and one of Olmsted's best-designed urban parks. It consists of two sections of unequal size--the larger Country Park exploits the area's scenic natural beauty, and the smaller Ante-Park provides recreational facilities. The most prominent feature of the Country Park is "a lovely dale gently winding between low wooded slopes, giving a broad expanse of unbroken turf, lost in the distance under scattered trees" (F.L.Olmsted, Sr.). The original plan for the Ante-Park featured a long promenade or mall ("The Greeting"), a deer park, a zoo for native animals, and a thirty-acre Playstead containing numerous athletic fields and a terrace along one side for seating, of which only the Playstead was realized. Each of the two sections of the park has its own circulation system, and they connect at the central Valley Gate. Simple rustic structures of stone and thatch originally dotted the park, and, although they no longer survive, efforts to replace them are underway. In 1911 Arthur A. Shurcliff designed an extensive area around the Greeting that was only partially constructed.

In 1990 Franklin Park underwent comprehensive long-range master planning as part of the Massachusetts Department of Environmental Management's Olmsted Historic Preservation program. The Halvorson Company was chosen to prepare the master plan, which it did with the aid of historical research and public input. The master plan calls for phased restoration and maintenance and the enhancement of the park's recreational opportunities. In 1992 this project won the BSLA award for Landscape Planning.

CITY OF BOSTON — PARK COMMISSION
GENERAL PLAN OF
FRANKLIN PARK
1881

In 1990 a Halvorson design integrated a running course and bridle path into the one-hundred-acre wilderness section of the park. Following natural topographic and vegetative features, the paths minimize their impact upon the landscape visually and environmentally while providing users with a varied and interesting experience. Lost features such as cobblestone gutters and an abandoned roadway have been uncovered and reused.

Johansson and Walcavage redesigned the park's Tiffany Moore and Walnut Avenue play lots to better integrate children's play into the surrounding natural environment. The playgrounds are organic in shape and use natural materials such as timber, sand, and rocks. New plantings in fluid shapes buffer the play areas from a nearby street. The design encourages children to explore the natural rock outcroppings, trees, and hills of the park. This design won a BSLA Merit Award in 1996 and a certificate for design excellence from the Massachusetts Horticultural Society in 1998.

Schoolmaster Hill was restored according to a plan developed by Pressley Associates in 1995. Olmsted's 265 foot long trellis-covered stone terrace was featured in the restoration plan.

*C*harlestown

Tourists on the Freedom Trail wishing to stop and rest between the U.S.S. Constitution and Bunker Hill will find a pleasant place in City Square Park. The fountain is the park's focus, but sculpture and interpretive signage describing Charlestown's history add interest. More than seventy-five species of deciduous and evergreen trees grow in the park, making it colorful in all seasons. Traditional building materials – brick, granite, cast iron, bronze – create a sense of unity with this neighborhood that dates from 1629. This project received a BSLA Merit Award in 1997.

City Square Park (58)

Bounded by Main, City Square, and Chelsea Streets, and Rutherford Avenue, Charlestown

The Halvorson Company

59 Shipyard Park

Charlestown Navy Yard,
Charlestown

Childs, Bertman, Tseckares,
and Casendino (CBT)

The work on Shipyard Park was the first step in the Boston Redevelopment Authority's revitalization plan for Boston's historic harbor complex. The park was planned as a symbol of change and improvement in an abandoned and desolate industrial environment. The CBT plan features a gentle landscape with rolling mounds and plantings to contrast with the hard surfaces of the surrounding historic industrial structures. The park features a large fountain with terraced pools and flowing water and an amphitheater that shelters people from the wind and allows a great view of the downtown skyline. The success of this park helped to induce redevelopment, and the design has received two awards: a national landscape award from the American Association of Nurserymen in 1981 and a Landscape Design Award from *Timberform* Magazine in 1980.

Established in the early 1800's, the Navy Yard in Charlestown was one of the city's chief employers until recent times, producing more than 35 warships between 1825 and 1868 and repairing ships in dry-dock during the first and second world wars. Part of a multi-phase redevelopment project, the waterfront promenade known as Shipyard Park sits adjacent to the U.S.S. Constitution National Historic Site, home of "old Ironsides." Shipyard Park incorporates artifacts of Boston's maritime history, such as anchors and the crane and rails used for the ship repair in the drydock. The durable wooden walkway was designed to withstand heavy public use and salt spray and to respect the industrial character of the Navy Yard's past.

60 Shipyard Park, Phase III

Charlestown Navy Yard,
Charlestown

Brown and Rowe

61 Shipyard Quarters, Piers 6 and 7

Charlestown Navy Yard,
First Avenue, Charlestown

Carol R. Johnson Associates

Carol R. Johnson Associates redeveloped Piers 6 and 7 at the Shipyard Quarters within the former Navy Yard into a recreational promenade and marina with viewing platforms, seating, and sun canopies. Public promenade areas feature gated access to the marina and offer panoramic views of historic Boston Harbor and the Boston skyline.

This park is one of the best surviving examples of Olmsted's early neighborhood playground designs in Boston. Recent master planning and design efforts by Walker-Kluesing focused on restoring the park's historic image and increasing passive recreational opportunities. Traditional plantings, benches, lighting, and a shade pavilion are all part of the plan. Three sets of serpentine granite steps, as detailed in the original Olmsted plan, were reconstructed during the north slope restoration.

Doherty Playground (62)
Charlestown Heights, Charlestown

Frederick Law Olmsted Sr.; Walker-Kluesing Design Group

The Warren Prescott Schoolyard was the first schoolyard constructed under the City of Boston's Schoolyard Initiative. The design process involved students, teachers, and the community, and the new design of the schoolyard incorporated these various groups' visions and needs. The playground includes outdoor space for ceremonial events, graphics for education and play, a play structure, and an area for special needs children. Educational materials were provided to the teachers about all of the plants that were used on the grounds – the cherry trees, for example, are the same type as those planted on the Washington Mall which were a gift from the people of Japan to the United States. The design of the Warren Prescott Schoolyard earned a BSLA Merit Award for Parks and Recreation in 1997.

Warren Prescott Schoolyard (63)
Pearl Street, Charlestown

Wallace Floyd Associates

*E*ast Boston

East Boston Piers Park is the largest waterfront park north of New York Harbor. It provides recreational opportunities to visitors along a six-hundred-foot promenade, as well as full views of both the downtown Boston skyline and the harbor. Both native and salt-tolerant plants compose the park's extensive plantings. A sailing center within the park is decorated with maritime symbols, and shade pavilions give visitors a place to relax. The park was designed through a collaborative process involving state agencies and community groups. It received the 1998 Excellence on the Waterfront award by the Waterfront Center in Washington, D.C., and a BSLA Merit Award for Park Design in 1996.

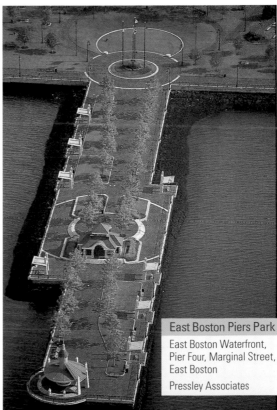

East Boston Piers Park (64)
East Boston Waterfront, Pier Four, Marginal Street, East Boston

Pressley Associates

The Harborwalk at Logan International Airport
(65)
One Harborside Drive,
Logan Airport, Boston
Carol R. Johnson Associates

This linear park is a one-mile-long path which follows the curving shoreline of Boston Harbor. At various locations the path widens into plazas with seating that allow walkers to enjoy the ferry and fire-boat docking areas and experience scenic views of Boston Harbor and the skyline.

Logan Airport Hilton
(66)
East Boston
The Halvorson Company

This hotel site, which travelers see as they emerge from the Ted Williams Tunnel, serves as a visual gateway for the Logan Airport terminal. In Phase 1 of the project, completed in 1999, the landscape blends contemporary forms with vernacular materials such as dry laid stone walls and native plantings that introduce visitors arriving in Boston to the New England region.

Hugh Roe O'Donnell Schoolyard
(67)
Lexington Street, East Boston
John Copley Associates/
Lynn Wolff Associates

The renovation of the O'Donnell School in East Boston transformed an asphalt-covered lot into a colorful schoolyard. The area now showcases a children's arboretum, two play structures, a story-telling area, an educational garden, and painted game graphics. Children's art is a focus for the schoolyard, with drawings enameled onto tiles set into curved concrete seatwalls, and images of sea creatures attached to a wavy fence with a sun-shaped arched gateway. The marine motif of the fence hints at East Boston's origin as an island in the harbor. The project received an Urban Landscape Award from the Massachusetts Historical Society in 1996 and an award from the Boston Society of Landscape Architects in 1999 for Institutional Design.

Eagle Hill Memorial Community Garden
(68)
Border Street
Cortes Associates with
Francis Fox Spinks Associates

This project transformed a vacant lot into a community gardening and gathering space, providing a valuable commodity to the neighborhood while also improving the visual character of the streetscape. The slope of the site made it necessary to terrace the area by constructing retaining walls. Special raised planters were built for elderly and handicapped gardeners. In 1994 this project received a BSLA Award for Parks and Recreation.

Nicknamed the "Sapphire Necklace," the Harborwalk will eventually be a 43.5-mile-long stretch of uninterrupted pathway along Boston's inner Harbor. (Currently about half of the walk is accessible.) This pedestrian path along the waterfront was envisioned in the spirit of Olmsted's Emerald Necklace, the band of interconnected parks and open space that runs through the center of the city. Some of the "jewels" in the Sapphire Necklace include Ventura Park, Belle Isle Salt Marsh, the Charles River Locks, and Commercial Wharf. In addition to linking significant sights, the Harborwalk will provide recreational opportunities and excellent skyline and waterfront views.

The courthouse on Boston's Fan Pier has spectacular views of downtown Boston and the harbor. An 800-foot promenade links this site to the Harborwalk (an extensive network of trails that provides access to the waterfront). Development ideas for the promenade area include a water shuttle service, guided tour boats, quiet areas for contemplation, and an educational garden with plantings that show the natural progression from seaside to upland ecosystems.

This waterfront site features the Seaport Hotel and a two-story plaza that provides a pedestrian link to nearby Commonwealth Pier that has convention and exhibition facilities. The upper plaza is constructed on a deck with parking below and includes a landscaped "outdoor room" extending from the Grand Ballroom of the hotel. Plants were selected for their ability to tolerate seaside conditions, and care was taken to ensure tree planting pits did not contact saline ground water.

Northern Avenue was historically important in maintaining the commercial activity of the industrial waterfront; today it is being revitalized as the backbone of a new commercial district focused on the World Trade Center. The future Eastport Park is part of the revitalization effort and will cover an underground parking facility. When finished in 2000, the park will have curvilinear paths, a winter-garden structure, a pergola, an obelisk, a grotto, and a harbor overlook.

This waterfront park is the primary pedestrian open space for Marine Industrial Park on Boston Harbor and accommodates a variety of passive recreational uses. The park reflects the geometric forms of nearby industry—a linear tree planting and pedestrian pathway mirror the huge rows of silos on the industrial harbor skyline. Other plantings frame views of the harbor and establish comfortable pedestrian areas. In 1988 the project received an Honor Award in the National Waterfront Center's "Excellence on the Waterfront" competition.

South Boston - Harborfront

The Harborwalk
Boston Harborfront
Boston Redevelopment Authority

United States Federal Court House (70)
One Courthouse Way, Fan Pier
Carol R. Johnson Associates;
Olin Partnership

World Trade Center/ Seaport Hotel/ Northern Avenue Master Plan (71)
Northern Avenue between B and D Streets, Boston
The Halvorson Company

Pier 10 Park (72)
End of Dry Dock Avenue, South Boston
The Halvorson Company

People passing historic Lewis Wharf along the Harborwalk will encounter Cella Park, a beautiful restoration of a once rugged industrial site. The park offers scenic views of Boston Harbor and the Boston Sailing Center. Using New England gray granite and recycled brick, the park harmonizes with the surrounding environment and evokes some of the ruggedness of its past. Plantings were selected for their ability to tolerate the windy and salty shoreline environment. The project was awarded the Urban Landscape Award of the Massachusetts Horticultural Society in 1998.

(73) Cella Park and Harborwalk

Lewis Wharf at Atlantic Avenue and Commercial Street, Boston

The Halvorson Company

(74) Castle Island Playground

Castle Island, Boston Harbor, Boston

Wallace, Floyd, Associates

This was the first playground to be redesigned according to the Metropolitan District Commission's master plan for its 52 playgrounds throughout the city. Located on Castle Island in Boston Harbor, the playground relates to its historic and natural environment, and won a BSLA Park Design Award for this in 1995. It takes the shape of Fort Independence, a pentagon with projecting bastions that provide children of different ages with separate play areas. Etched steel plaques containing information about the fort's history create a game around the playground perimeter, combining education and recreation.

(75) South Boston Beaches Restoration

South Boston

Carol R. Johnson Associates

The public beaches along this three-mile stretch are connected by a "strandway," or boulevard, designed by the Olmsted office around the turn of the century. Historic landscape designs along the strandway include Olmsted's Marine Park at Pleasure Bay, the bandstand, and the Mother's Rest Pavilion, all of which have already been restored.

*R*oxbury

Originally used as a railroad line and then proposed to become an expressway, the Southwest Corridor sliced through the city and separated communities. Following vigorous protest it became a 5 mile long, 55-acre park – the largest park project in Boston since Olmsted's Emerald Necklace. Southwest Corridor Park is a recreational arterial passing through several neighborhoods, responding to the unique needs of each and containing such features as play yards and community gardens. Its continuity is maintained with a double-wide pathway, one pedestrian, one bicycle, and rows of trees. Granite from a former rampart was recycled and used throughout the corridor. Users can access the park from numerous entrances, and so the corridor that once separated neighborhoods now helps to connect them. The park project received an ASLA Merit Award 1979.

Southwest Corridor Park (76)

Roxbury, Jamaica Plain,
Back Bay, Boston

Roy Mann Associates;
Moreice and Gary (Back Bay);
Carol R. Johnson and Associates
(Ruggles Street Station);
Mason and Frey (Forest Hills);
Huygens and DeMella
(Jackson Square Station)

This public park features the Dillaway Thomas House, an eighteenth-century Georgian home reputed to be the headquarters for General John Thomas of the Continental Army during the Revolutionary War. After its an award-winning restoration in 1992, the home now gives interpretive tours and contains space for exhibits. Other historical aspects of the park include the creation of a new orchard honoring the development of the Roxbury Russet apple, the recreation of medicinal herb gardens that were cultivated on the site, and the preservation of a foundation wall from a previously existing building. The park also has an amphitheater and lawn areas for performances, a toddler playground, and an all-weather telescope.

**Roxbury Heritage
State Park** (77)

Roxbury

Massachusetts Department of
Environmental Management

(78)	Dudley Town Common
	John Copley and Associates/ Lynn Wolff Associates

The Dudley Town Common is a lively public center with many uses, serving as a community gateway and an open space for public gatherings and performances. The artwork and the park improvements capture multicultural and historical aspects of the community and encourage young and old to gather here. These improvements include ceramic animal benches and a variety of interpretive elements such as a "history fence," a "music fence," and a "Bill of Rights seatwall." Neighborhood residents formed a design review committee which played a key role in the development of the park. In 1996 this project received the BSLA Merit Award for Park and Recreational Facilities Design as well as the Massachusetts Horticultural Award for Urban Landscapes. In 1997 it received the Willo Von Moltke Urban Design Award from the Boston Society of Architects.

(79)	Holborn Street Totlot Renovation
	Roxbury
	John Copley Associates/ Lynn Wolff Associates

This colorful neighborhood playground has become a gathering spot for the surrounding community, and is the result of a successful design process that included substantial public input. The playground includes a children's spray fountain, play structures, decorative fencing, and a steel arch gateway that incorporates drawings done by neighborhood children and thus fosters a sense of stewardship and personal responsibility toward the park. The project received the Urban Landscape Award from the Massachusetts Horticultural Society in 1997.

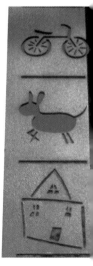

(80)	Ruggles Plaza and Streetscape
	800 Columbus Avenue, Boston
	Carol R. Johnson Associates; The Halvorson Company

This station was constructed in 1987 as part of the Orange Line subway relocation. Future additions were anticipated at the time, so temporary landscaping was installed which can be removed to accommodate growth.

A five-acre development along the Southwest Corridor next to the Ruggles MBTA station has a garden that can accommodate active as well as passive recreation. Future plans include five more buildings organized cohesively around a new roadway.

A 1997 BSLA Merit Award winner, the redevelopment of this existing housing complex reduced the density of units and created a townhouse-style environment, better integrating it with its neighborhood. New streets were added, the landscape was extensively redesigned, and the buildings got front and rear courtyards, all of which tended to give each unit a discrete identity. Many of the ideas came from the tenant association, which played an integral part in the design process.

Residents of Grant Manor Housing were an important part of the design process, and they inspired many of the ideas for improvements. Plans include the creation of play areas within sight of the units and outdoor areas for sitting, relaxing, and picnicking. In addition the plans call for widening the decorative brick pathways to the buildings' main entrances and de-emphasizing the secondary entrances with plant screenings so as to clarify pedestrian traffic. New plantings of trees and shrubs will reinforce existing plantings to create a feeling of enclosure and community throughout the site.

*D*orchester

The JFK Library, designed by I. M. Pei, sits prominently at Columbia Point on Boston Harbor, the site of a former landfill. To tolerate the severe seaside conditions and to remember President Kennedy, hardy plants from Cape Cod were brought to the site: Beach Plum, Northern Bayberry, Rugosa Rose, and Japanese Black Pine, among others. The landscape's major trees are planted in blocks and rows to act as windbreaks. Kennedy's sailboat, the Victura, along with two areas for picnicking and access to a linear waterfront park, are prominent features of this park.

The Harbor Point Housing revitalization project laid out a central mall running through Harbor Point—a green spine that unifies the entire development. The mall affords scenic views of the harbor islands. Play areas provide additional recreational opportunities for residents. And the addition of front and back yards has created a small neighborhood atmosphere.

85 Old Harbor Park

Mount Vernon Street,
Dorchester

Carol R. Johnson Associates

The comprehensive modernization program for the Harbor Point housing community included the creation of Old Harbor Park, a one-mile linear waterfront park. This park connects to a larger Boston Harbor trail system and offers spectacular views of the water and the JFK Library. The trail connecting the park to the Harbor Point housing project has a terrace that extends over the water. The trail itself has many unique features. People on the trail can see the harbor islands; there are steps leading to the water's edge; it has a pocket beach for bathing; and interpretive signage along the way describes the history and geography of the park. In 1993 the project received a BSLA award.

Dorchester Heights is the site of a Revolutionary War fortification, which forced British troops to evacuate Boston on March 17, 1776. The site

86 Dorchester Heights Monument and Thomas Park

Dorchester

Child Associates; Lynn Wolff Associates; Cynthia Zaitzevsky

was developed as a public park area and the South Boston Reservoir in the mid-19th Century and was designated as the Dorchester Heights National Historic Site in 1951. A cultural landscape report completed by Child Associates, Inc. with Lynn Wolff Associates Inc. and historian Cynthia Zaitzevsky, established the historical significance of Dorchester Heights/Thomas Park and recommended treatment and design to improve the function of the cultural landscape, while preserving features that are important in defining its significance.

Jamaica Plain

87 Temple Israel

260 Riverway, Boston

The Architects Collaborative

A 1975 addition to Temple Israel created three new exterior spaces—a garden plaza, a children's garden, and a biblical garden—and a bluestone plaza makes the transition between the Temple and the gardens. Wooden terraces in the children's garden are part of the play area and can be climbed on. In the biblical garden identifying signage for plants gives common, Latin, and Hebrew names as well as biblical references. In 1988 this project received a BSLA Merit Award for Mature Projects.

88 Forbes Street Community Garden

19-31 Forbes Street
Jamaica Plain, Boston

Boston Natural Areas Fund; Forbes Street Community Gardeners; Cortés Associates

This garden occupies a broad slope in the streetcar suburb of Jamaica Plain. A contaminated, derelict, residential site until the 1990s, this community garden was developed and built through the collaborative work of neighbors and nonprofit organizations with the city. Salvaged granite blocks were used to create a series of stepped terraces to make the area workable for gardening. When the soil was found to have high lead levels and had to be detoxified in order to meet Massachusetts State environmental standards, the garden project raised public

awareness of the hazards of lead in the soil throughout the city and became a spur for lead abatement strategies in many other community gardens. A place for growing one's own food and meeting neighbors, this garden has been a rallying point for community renewal.

One-hundred-fifty-year-old Forest Hills Cemetery is one of the nation's largest and most beautiful burial grounds. It was created by Henry Dearborn, who also worked on nearby Mount Auburn Cemetery. Forest Hills is a rural garden cemetery designed in the English picturesque style. The layout suggests an idyllic rural town with winding streets and romantic street names. Many nineteenth-century Bostonians delighted in coming here on the weekends for picnics and pleasure outings to escape the noise and dirt of the city. In designing nearby Franklin Park, Frederick Law Olmsted may well have looked to Forest Hills for inspiration.

The cemetery's unique landscape consists of a series of glacial drumlins, which provide dramatic settings for terraces and scenic vistas. Tree and shrub plantings throughout the cemetery—copper and cutleaf beech, Japanese umbrella pine, false cypress, sequoia, and such—create a romantic, peaceful aura. The cemetery's fine collection of Victorian sculpture includes works by Daniel Chester French, Martin Milmore, and Anna Coleman Ladd. Visitors can find the graves of Eugene O'Neil, Anne Sexton, and e. e. cummings, to name but a few famous literary figures who are buried here.

Snowflake Hill and the beautiful stone bell tower at its summit are prominent landmarks at the main entrance to historic Forest Hills Cemetery. Brown and Rowe researched historical data and old photographs of the area to prepare a landscape management plan which focused on preserving the natural character of Snowflake Hill by caring for the existing mature trees and shrubs, opening up views to the bell tower, and highlighting the puddingstone ledge.

Located in a densely populated urban neighborhood, this park meets the needs of many different users. It includes playground equipment designed for use by children of various ages, a spray wall for interactive water play, and seating areas. The park design fosters a sense of community ownership and reduces the likelihood of future vandalism by incorporating art works such as a graffiti panel created by neighborhood residents. In 1992, the project received a BSLA Merit Award for Urban Design.

*B*rookline

Charles Platt, one of America's foremost early landscape architects, helped to design the Weld Estate. It is an unusual work for Platt because of its separation of the house and the garden by both a pinetum, a thickly planted grove of pine trees, and a bowling green in the Italian tradition of *giardino segreto.* Platt conceived of the garden here as an outdoor room, and filled it with architecture and furniture, such as fountains, pergola, statuary, benches, and urns. Until its recent restoration the estate, now Larz Anderson Park, had been in decline for many years. It is listed on the National Register of Historic Places and contains a carriage house occupied by the Museum of Transportation, specimen trees, and remnants of the gardens designed by Platt. Situated high on a glacial drumlin, the park offers excellent views in many directions. Master planning and design work by Walker-Kluesing focused on restoring the historic features and increasing recreational opportunities, for which the firm won awards from the Massachusetts Historical Commission and the BSLA in 1992.

(91) **Larz Anderson Park, Weld Estate**

Newton Street, Brookline

Charles Platt;
Walker-Kluesing Design Group

(92) **Fairsted, The Frederick Law Olmsted National Historic Site**

99 Warren Street, Brookline

Frederick Law Olmsted Sr.;
John Charles Olmsted; Shary
Page Berg; Cynthia Zaitzevsky;
Carol R. Johnson Associates;
National Park Service

The former home and office of Frederick Law Olmsted Sr. is now owned and operated by the National Park Service. In the 1880s Olmsted and his sons transformed the Fairsted property into a classic example of his domestic landscape ideals: they employed elements such as a picturesque hollow and rock garden, a small pastoral greensward, and numerous vine-covered structures. In the 1980s the National Park Service managed various projects including landscape improvements directed by Shary Page Berg and the development of a trellis system to support the historic vines on the house. In addition, the Olmsted Center for Landscape Preservation and the Olmsted National Historic Site have largely completed a circa-1930 landscape restoration. Among the many collaborators on this work are the Arnold Arboretum of Harvard University, Cynthia Zaitzevsky, and Carol R. Johnson Associates.

(93) **Corey Hill Park**

Summit Avenue,
Town of Brookline

John F. Furlong

A walk up Summit Avenue from Olmsted's Beacon Street to this hilltop park will reward you with spectacular views of Boston, Cambridge, and Brookline. Sitting walls of curved stone define the crest of the hill and enclose a small playground on the west side. A sundial plaza on the east side allows visitors to mark the time of day with their own shadow. It is a site for memorable sunsets at any time of year. In the winter the park becomes a sledder's paradise.

Longwood Area

This quadrangle is an important example of campus design that came out of the City Beautiful movement of the early 1900s. The original architects were Shepley, Rutan, and Coolidge In 1989 Harvard constructed a parking facility beneath the main quadrangle. In collaboration with the Massachusetts Historical Commission, Pressley Associates restored the quadrangle according to the Olmsted Brothers' 1905 planting plan.

Harvard Medical School Main Quadrangle (94)
Longwood Avenue, Boston
Olmsted Brothers;
Pressley Associates

Located in the historic Longwood Medical Area of Boston, this hospital was renovated including its entry area as well as building additions which created roof deck space. The entry drive, drop-off, and parking are organized around a central allee of trees, and a gateway at the street edge which uses similar materials and architectural motifs as the hospital building. A system of precast planter boxes specially designed for the roof deck enlivens the space, which also contains plants providing year-round interest and two ceremonial lanterns inspired by older, existing ones.

Longwood Medical Research Center  (95)
221 Longwood Avenue, Boston
John Copley and Associates

The public plaza of the Clinical Center echoes the art deco detailing of this landmark hospital building. A promenade with walkways, plazas, and parterres beneath bosquets of shade trees stretches along the main façade while tree plantings shelter a café and create intimate spaces for visitors. Patterns developed with various pavement materials reflect the textures and colors of the art deco façade, unifying building and site. It is a winner of the BSLA Award for Institutional Design in 1996.

The Clinical Center, Beth Israel Hospital (96)
Brookline Avenue, Boston
Child Associates

Space for two new courtyards was created through a recent addition to the hospital. These courtyards provide a visual focus for the lobby, and they contain viewing gardens that promote a calming environment for staff and patients. The gardens, visible from many directions and levels, provide multi-season interest. Colonnades of ginkgoes and columnar oaks with rows of hollies and crabapples recall the porticoes of an ancient atrium. The central gardens are planted in an informal, naturalistic manner with blueberry, azalea, and Japanese snowbell and provide an unexpected contrast with the ordered spaces around them. In 1990 this project received a BSLA Merit Award for Institutional Design.

New England Baptist Hospital Courtyards 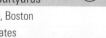 (97)
Pilgrim Road, Boston
Child Associates

The Children's Hospital Gateway Park and Winter Garden

300 Longwood Avenue, Boston

Walker-Kluesing Design Group

As its name suggests, this two-level park serves as a gateway and main entrance to the hospital. The lower-level street garden contains seating and ornamental lion's heads to entertain children, while the roof garden above contains a lawn balcony for relaxing and playing. Both levels are edged with rhododendrons, ivy, and dogwood, so the design creates an attractive double band of green facing the street.

The Winter Garden is an open-air courtyard, the visual heart of the hospital. Colorful plantings set against a backdrop of white birch trees enliven the space. The garden supports the unique needs of families in a medical environment by providing comfortable places for them to relax. In 1990 this project received a BSLA Merit Award for Institutional Design.

New England Deaconess Hospital

Brookline Avenue, Boston

Walker-Kluesing Design Group

The hospital's inviting main entrance faces the recently upgraded Joslin Park. The park gives the area a comfortable residential feeling, and that feeling is continued into the main lobby through the use of lush plantings. A playground facility for the hospital's daycare recently moved to a safer, more convenient location. The design received both the Honor Award for Modern Healthcare from the AIA and the Design Excellence Award from the BSA/AIA in 1995.

Formerly a parking lot, this prominent site on the Wentworth Institute of Technology campus has been transformed into a public greenspace and athletic fields. Extensive plantings soften the surrounding urban environment and welcome visitors, while the use of brick piers and wrought iron fencing around the playing fields visually links them with the existing structures on campus. An innovative drainage system allows the athletic fields to act as an aquifer recharge area, and the synthetic turf and retractable ball containment system represent state-of-the-art technology.

Myles Elliott and Eugenia Louise Sweeney Field

Wentworth Institute of Technology
500 Huntington Avenue, Boston

Carol R. Johnson Associates

West Roxbury – Allston – Brighton

This ninety-two-acre site located on the Charles River is being transformed from a landfill into a public park and is scheduled for completion in November 2000. The project is sponsored by the mayor's office, an appointed citizen's advisory committee, and the City Public Works and Parks Departments. It will include active and passive recreation with over twenty acres of multi-purpose playing fields; a children's play area; two-and-a-half miles of walking and jogging paths; nature study areas; a canoe launch; picnic areas; extensive plantings, including native grasses; and parking for over 350 vehicles. The park will be linked to the Metropolitan District Commission's Brook Farm and other open spaces along the Charles River.

Gardner Street Park

Gardner Street, off
VFW Parkway, West Roxbury

Camp Dresser and McKee
with Brown and Rowe

This urban housing project had deteriorated badly before it underwent complete reconstruction, for which it won a BSLA Merit Award for Multi-Family Housing in 1987. Three new community facilities were built, as well as a new "private" street which contributes to the look of a more traditional residential development. Other changes included the addition of toddler playgrounds, children's play areas, public gathering space, car washing areas, community gardens, and front and rear entrances for each apartment. Public and private spaces are delineated through the use of grading, fencing, and plantings, and these changes help to instill ownership responsibilities for the outdoor spaces.

Commonwealth Development

Commonwealth Avenue
and Fidelis Way, Brighton

Philip E. Pryor and
Katherine A. Schreiber

The master plan for this eight-and-a-half-acre site includes two buildings (one of which will be the future corporate headquarters) and a parking garage. The plan calls for an elevated courtyard with seating walls, plantings, and red brick paving unifying the buildings and the surrounding grounds. Through the expanded use of sidewalks, grassy open spaces, and street tree plantings, the current building has been carefully integrated with its two distinguished neighbors: the Harvard Business School and the National Historic District of the Charles River Reservation.

Genzyme Corporation Biopharmaceutical Manufacturing Plant

500 Soldiers Field Road, Allston

Carol R. Johnson Associates

As part of their plan to eliminate vehicular traffic from campus, the Harvard Business School has begun transforming areas such as the Gallatin Hall grounds into pedestrian spaces. Attractive paving and new sitting areas have been added. New shrub and tree plantings, complementing an existing elm-lined walkway, provide visual interest year round.

Gallatin Hall (104)

Harvard Business School
Soldiers Field Road at
North Harvard Street, Boston

Carol R. Johnson Associates

The planting and site improvement effort around Chase Hall centered around enhancement of the entry courtyard, upgrading the irrigation system, and restoring all areas damaged by construction in the early 1980's.

Chase Hall (105)

Harvard Business School, Boston

Carol R. Johnson Associates

(106) Harvard Square

Massachusetts Avenue/
Brattle Street, Cambridge

Pressley Associates

Harvard Square, the cultural and retail center of Cambridge, is known locally as "The Hub of the Universe." During the 1960s it was undistinguished and dominated by car traffic. The square underwent major redesign in association with an extension of the MBTA Red Line subway, and vehicular and pedestrian traffic was completely reconfigured. The square was enhanced through the use of durable and historic building materials—granite, brick, and cast iron—as well as new lighting and shade tree plantings, all of which contribute to a lively pedestrian environment.

(107) Winthrop Park

Kennedy Street, Cambridge

Brown and Rowe

This site, originally established as Newtowne Marketplace in 1631, has been used continuously as a public space for three and a half centuries. Its restoration as a 19th century town green allows it to serve as an important open space link between Harvard Square and the Charles River, providing much needed green space in this dense urban environment. Sculptor Carlos Dorrien designed a piece specifically for the site. In 1988 this project won the BSLA Honor Award for Park, Recreation and Open Space design.

(108) John Fitzgerald Kennedy Memorial Park

Memorial Drive, Cambridge

Carol R. Johnson Associates

This park is part of the Charles River Reservation and is an important pedestrian link to Harvard Square. The park's focus, along the axis of the pedestrian way, is a fountain memorial constructed of granite that sends smooth sheets of water falling over polished walls. Quotations from President John F. Kennedy's speeches are inscribed on the walls. The five-acre park is landscaped with plants that bloom in May around the time of JFK's birthday. The project received a Merit Award from the BSLA in 1995.

Winner of the 1987 BSLA Merit Award for Commercial Design, Charles Square is a mixed-use complex containing hotels, retail and office spaces, and condominium development. Stepped terraces and courtyards create an open link to Harvard Square and provide a focus for the project's many activities. These elements, along with plantings similar to others in the area and carefully selected building and paving materials, integrate this new development into its urban setting.

Charles Square (109)
1 Bennett Street, Cambridge
The SWA Group

This comprehensive urban redesign project at Quincy Square transformed a vast expanse of asphalt at the intersection of five streets into an attractive pedestrian environment. The centerpiece of this area is a small park prominently located on Massachusetts Avenue near Harvard University. Quincy Square consists of a spiral laid out according to the golden mean with a large stone and bronze boulder at its center. This visually distinctive design is enhanced through rich plantings of hardy perennials, ornamental grasses, shade trees, and flowering shrubs that are tolerant of the urban stresses of this high-traffic area. The project received a Merit Award from the BSLA in 1998.

Quincy Square (110)
Massachusetts Avenue at
Quincy and Bow Streets, Cambridge
The Halvorson Company;
David Phillips, Sculptor

Longfellow National Historic Site

105 Brattle Street, Cambridge

Martha Brooks Hutcheson;
Ellen Biddle Shipman;
Diane Kostial McGuire;
National Park Service

This historic house and site occupy two acres near Harvard Square and the Charles River in Cambridge. The house served as George Washington's headquarters during the early months of the Revolutionary War (1775-76). In the mid 1800's the poet Henry Wadsworth Longfellow lived here, contributing to the layout of the grounds, particularly the visual link with the Charles River. His daughter Alice continued the tradition achieving prominence as a national example of the Colonial Revival style through the formal garden designed by Martha Brooks Hutcheson and Ellen Biddle Shipman. In 1970, Diane Kostial McGuire made plans for the gardens that were partially implemented. The National Park Service is currently planning a rehabilitation to improve public access and to establish a more compatible historic appearance.

University Green

130-132 Mt. Auburn Street, Cambridge

Carol R. Johnson Associates

This multiple-award winning project site was designed in the style of a mid-1800s urban neighborhood, but with a twist—it is located above an underground parking structure. Designers had to contend with challenging drainage and structural limitations, but with guidance from two preservation organizations, over fifty condominium units were built and integrated with existing restored buildings. Beautiful plantings feature species from a typical 1850s urban garden and help to blend old and new.

*H*arvard University

Harvard Yard – Master Plan

Harvard Campus, Cambridge

Michael Van Valkenburgh

The primary impetus for the renovation of this landscape was the death of its elm trees. The new planting scheme replaces the elm monoculture with several varieties of trees. The canopy of trees acts as a ceiling and the groundplane as a floor, which together create a volumetric space enclosing and unifying the many disparate styles of architecture within the yard. This sensitive redesign adds something new while retaining what Van Valkenburgh calls the "frugal elegance" of the yard.

Located in a heavily trafficked intersection on the Harvard campus, Tanner Fountain is a circular arrangement of 159 granite fieldstones set in asphalt and grass, integrating a misting fountain. In the spring, summer, and fall the fountain's jets spray water mist, and in the winter they release steam, thus providing year-round interest. The design invites both exploration and contemplation, and it reflects the mystery of primeval places as well as the rocky character of New England. In 1985 the project received a BSLA Merit Award for Institutional Design, and in 1987 it received an ASLA Honor Award.

Tanner Fountain (114)
Science Center,
Harvard University, Cambridge
The SWA Group and
Peter Walker

The urban garden for Quincy House is defined with brick terraces, walls, and fences. This was the first of several landscape designs by Sasaki Associates for Harvard University. Others include Leverett House, Peabody Terrace, and Holyoke Center. Sasaki also developed the plans for renovating paths, lighting, and plantings in Harvard Yard.

Quincy House (115)
Harvard University, Cambridge
Sasaki Associates

This one-acre urban infill site contains two interconnected dormitory buildings and an underground parking facility that has a landscaped roof deck. The architecture and landscape of the project respect both the Harvard campus vernacular and the surrounding residential neighborhood by featuring a double row of street trees and ornamental steel fencing with brick and granite piers. In addition, there are outdoor play areas for a children's day-care center and a vehicle drop-off area designed as a courtyard.

Harvard University's DeWolfe Street Housing (116)
DeWolfe Street, one half
block from Mt. Auburn Street,
Cambridge
The Halvorson Company

The campus landscape of the Harvard Law School features a curvilinear brick-edged walkway, providing north and south access to the campus. The brick for the edging matches that used for the building entrances and thus connects the space physically and visually. To avoid the use of retaining walls, the landscape architects created rolling green slopes and formed planted banks in the steepest areas.

Harvard Law School (117)
1563 Massachusetts Avenue,
Cambridge
Carol R. Johnson Associates

M^{IT -} Kendall Square

Massachusetts Institute of Technology McDermott Court

(118)

MIT, Cambridge

Sasaki Associates

MIT's new courtyard, the McDermott Court, was built to link the heart of the east campus with the Charles River, giving the campus a clear unifying form that it had lacked. Alexander Calder's monumental thirty-five-foot-tall walk-through sculpture "La Grande Voile" stands at its center.

(119)

University Park at MIT – Phase II

Massachusetts Avenue at Sidney Street Cambridge

The Halvorson Company

In the heart of historic Cambridgeport next to the MIT campus, University Park is a major mixed-use urban redevelopment. It includes a new hotel with a roof garden, retail development, and a park that sits at the entrance to the complex. The signature open space of this project is another park, the 1.3-acre University Park Common, that will serve as an entry to the entire redevelopment project. This park will help to integrate contemporary uses with the district's historic character.

(120)

Cambridge Center/ Kendall Square

Kendall Square, Cambridge

Carol R. Johnson Associates

Carol R. Johnson Associates, as part of a design team, prepared a report for the Cambridge Redevelopment Authority on guidelines and standards for landscape development at Cambridge Center, a new twenty-five-acre mixed-use corporate/commercial complex in Kendall Square. Guidelines addressed issues such as visitor orientation, integration of pedestrian and vehicular circulation, visual enrichment and appropriate scale, safety and security, environmental problems, convenience, and maintenance. The site improvements installed around the new office buildings are prototypical designs by Carol R. Johnson Associates and include pavement, lights, planting, and site furniture. The designs follow the guidelines and standards of the earlier CRJA studies. The completion of the project is estimated to cost $10 million in public funds.

In a fine example of community beautification, a fairly straightforward building relocation—moving the twelve-hundred-car parking garage on this site back from the street—created space for a striking perennial garden. The colors in the garden change weekly and are described in a garden bulletin distributed to the tenants of Cambridge Center. The project won the Massachusetts Horticultural Society's Urban Landscape Award and a BSLA Award in 1990.

Cambridge Center North Park *(121)*

Between Binney Street and Broadway, Kendall Square, Cambridge

Pressley Associates

This one-acre garden built over a parking garage provides a dramatic park setting in the midst of a high-rise mixed-use development. Strong winds and the limited load-bearing capacity of the structure forced the designers to create a garden without trees or shrubs. To simulate these traditional garden elements, SWA instead used materials such as metal trellises, wood planters, crushed stone, groundcovers, and vines. The result is a modern landscape of geometric parterres, mazes, and lattice-works, which won a BSLA Merit Award for Park Design in 1985 and an ASLA Merit Award in 1984.

Cambridge Center Garage Roof Garden *(122)*

Cambridge Center, Kendall Square, Cambridge

The SWA Group

(123) Biogen, Inc.
Kendall Square, Cambridge
Payette Associates

The focal point of this building is an exterior courtyard with three distinct spaces for both public and private uses. The three areas include entertainment and event space associated with the public lobby, an outdoor cafe, and a lower court with a fountain designed for private contemplation and relaxation. Each space within the courtyard is clearly defined, yet connections among them allow for the smooth flow of traffic. In 1996 this project received a BSLA Merit Award for Commercial Design.

(124) Newtowne Court
Bounded by Main, Portland, Windsor, and Washington Streets, Cambridge
Carol R. Johnson Associates

This multifamily housing site redesign is a 1997 BSLA Merit Award winner. The landscape architects created two plaza spaces that include game tables, a playground, and waterplay facilities, as well as open lawn and areas of shade. First-floor units have pleasant front-door street entrances, and a series of semiprivate courtyards creates a friendlier, more residential atmosphere. Designers and residents worked closely together to ensure that residents' concerns and ideas were addressed, and renovation was spread out over several years, allowing residents to remain in their homes.

*E*ast Cambridge

(125) Lechmere Canal Park
Cambridge Side Place, East Cambridge
Carol R. Johnson Associates

This multiple-award-winning park is an exemplary reclamation project, transforming an industrial site into a vibrant seven-and-a-half-acre city park. The design expresses the history of the Lechmere canal area while contributing to the city's revitalization. Throughout the park, art works and historic imagery are hidden within the landscape, encouraging visitors to explore, providing fresh experiences, and invoking the historic spirit of the place. A canal and fountain basin were reclaimed, creating a water park, also historically reminiscent. A permanent system to improve water quality in the canal also has been invisibly incorporated within the site.

This park provides the middle link in a sixteen-acre open space running through East Cambridge. Visually it ties Lechmere Canal Park to Front Park on the Charles River, and it helps to unify the surrounding buildings. The park features a tree-lined brick-and-granite promenade as well as delightful bronze relief plaques by artist Nancy Webb, which are built into the park's curbing and columns.

Neighborhood support made possible the transformation of Centanni Way, a one-block city street, into a unique multiple-use space. Its function as a combination of pedestrian way, public plaza, and performing arts space earned it a Merit Award from the BSLA in 1989. The design uses a simple terraced garden of floral parterres to create an outdoor theater. A vine-covered trellis serves as a stage backdrop, and the staircase of a neighboring building provides seating for an audience of four hundred. The space also functions as a gateway between older, more established neighborhoods to the west and newly developing areas to the east.

Bulfinch Square consists of the Bulfinch Building, the Old Superior Courthouse, and a courtyard which links the two. Care was taken to insure that the new buildings with their new uses would be compatible with the historic county government buildings. The central courtyard unifies the various parts of the square visually and provides access for new additions such as the Cambridge Multicultural Arts Center.

Cambridge/Watertown

Mount Auburn, the first large-scale public open space and the first rural garden cemetery in the United States, was established in 1831 as a collaboration between Jacob Bigelow, a physician, General Henry A. S. Dearborn, the founder of the Massachusetts Horticultural Society, and Alex Wadsworth, a civil engineer. The design prototype was French but was strongly influenced by the eighteenth-century picturesque landscape style. This blending of styles initiated by Mount Auburn was widely copied: Laurel Hill in Philadelphia, Greenwood in Brooklyn, and Forest Hills in Roxbury are only three of dozens of such cemeteries across the country.

Mount Auburn has an amazing diversity of topography and water features. A complex network of pathways meander through the landscape. A stone tower on top of a large hill provides one of the finest

views of Boston to be found in the region. In addition to unusual and unique artistic monuments, the cemetery also contains an excellent arboretum with over five hundred varieties of trees. It is a favorite location for urban bird watching.

In 1990 the Halvorson Company developed a comprehensive master plan that focused on dwindling land resources and on design and use guidelines for maintenance and preservation, for which it won BSLA and ASLA awards in 1993. Halvorson also designed two innovative prototypes for burial expansion that fit well with the cemetery's historic landscape: One of them, Vesper Path, is a simple granite curb edging that contains engraved text memorials, which from a distance blends with the cemetery's scenic and historic qualities. The other prototype, Willow Pond, includes a granite wall that serves as a gateway to the pond area and provides spaces for memorial engravings. The pond edge plantings recently have been restored to Halvorson's original design.

The redesign of the Willow Pond knoll by Thomas M. Paine and Julie Moir Messervy transformed a bare hilltop into a sheltered place for contemplation. The knoll features a large cast iron sculpture by Richard Duca, which is reached by sinuous paths reflecting the form of the sculpture. Low granite walls contain memorial inscriptions, and as the walls swirl inward they metamorphose into sitting walls that look outward to Willow Pond and the surrounding landscape.

Sasaki's Willow Garden crypts developed the cemetery's last unused portion of land while preserving its historical and aesthetic qualities. The crypts are of a similar scale and style to existing ones, and their layout follows preexisting curving paths. A newly designed, formal U-shaped courtyard faces outward toward the older parts of the cemetery and also itself forms a visual terminus. In 1986 this project received a BSLA Merit Award for Institutional Landscapes.

---

(130)
Buckingham, Browne, and Nichols New Athletic Facility
Cambridge
Child Associates

An inviting entry plaza extends the architecture of this new athletic facility into the surrounding landscape. Trees and lights complement the monumental gymnasium wall, providing human scale to the space. A south-facing sloping lawn links upper and lower entry walks and provides informal seating for the athletic fields. A master plan for the Buckingham, Browne, and Nichols school was recently completed in collaboration with Chan Krieger and Associates.

Map 3 – Boston-Metropolitan Area

Boston Harbor Islands

131. Boston Harbor Islands State Park
132. Spectacle Island
133. Deer Island Wastewater Treatment Facility
134. World's End

Boston Metropolitan Area

135. Pope John Paul II Park, Boston
136. Lower Neponset River Reservation, Boston
137. Boston College Campus Entrance, Boston
138. Blue Hills Reservation, Milton
139. Adams National Historic Site, Quincy
140. Marina Bay, Squantum, Quincy
141. Constitution Common & Quincy City Hall
142. The Eleanor Cabot Bradley Reservation, Canton
143. The Hunnewell Estate, Wellesley
144. Elmbank, Newton
145. Upper Charles River Master Plan and
     Phased Implementation, Watertown, Weston,
     Waltham, and Newton
146. Church of Jesus Christ of Latter-day Saints,
     Belmont
147. Beaver Brook Reservation, Belmont
148. Danehy Park, Cambridge
149. Jefferson Park, Cambridge
150. Porter Square MBTA Station, Cambridge
151. Arsenal Park, Watertown
152. Lyman Estate, The Vale , Waltham
153. Prospect Hill Park, Waltham
154. Bay Colony Corporate Center, Waltham
155. Gropius House, Lincoln
156. The Codman House, Lincoln
157. Walden Pond State Reservation, Concord
158. Sleepy Hollow Cemetery, Concord
159. Minute Man National Historical Park and
     Battle Road Trail, Concord and Lincoln
160. The Minute Man Bikeway, Arlington and
     Lexington

161. Arlington Memorial Park, Arlington
162. Saint Charles Boromeo Church, Woburn
163. Middlesex Fells Reservation, Malden
164. Mystic River Reservation, Medford
165. Bendetson Hall, Tufts University, Medford
166. Meyer Campus Center,
     Tufts University, Medford
167. Tisch Family Library,
     Tufts University, Medford
168. Woodstock and Osgood Parks, Medford
169. Davis Square and MBTA Station, Somerville
170. Davis Square to Alewife Linear Park,
     Somerville and Cambridge
171. The Mystics, Somerville
172. Bosson Park, Chelsea
173. Mary C. Burke Elementary School,
     Chelsea
174. Revere Beach Reservation and
     Master Plan, Revere
175. Saugus Iron Works, Saugus
176. High Rock, Lynn

(above) Mayer Campus Center, Tufts University;
(left) Jefferson Park; (below) The Lyman Estate.

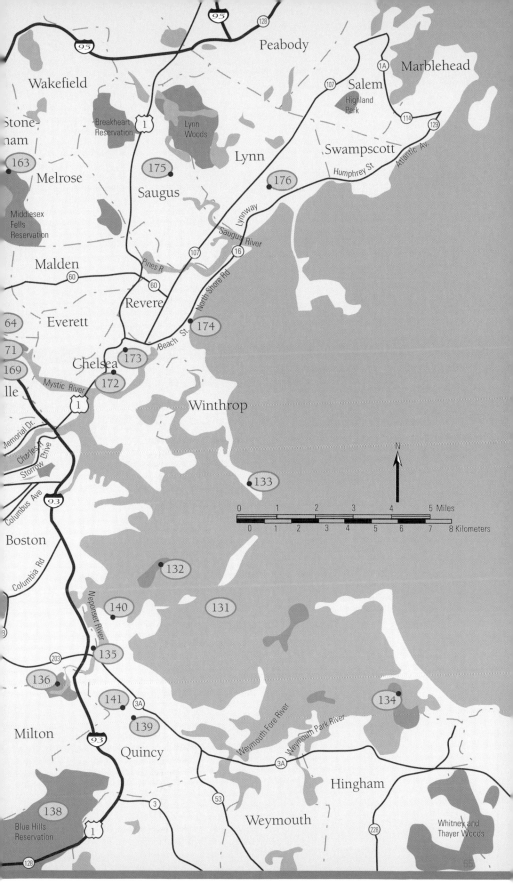

*B*oston Harbor Islands

(131) Boston Harbor Islands State Park

Boston, Hingham, and Weymouth

Walker-Kluesing Design Group

The Boston Harbor Islands have a unique environment and microclimate, and landscape design of these isolated places encourages people to visit and explore. Visitors to the islands can take advantage of shade trellises that provide protection from wind, rain, and sun and make a comfortable waiting area for the water taxi service. Constructed of heavy timbers and rough textured cedar shingles, these trellises blend with the pier and are in keeping with the New England vernacular style. Vista clearings along the trails crossing the island invite views of the harbor and downtown Boston, while new indigenous plantings shelter exposed areas.

(132) Spectacle Island

Spectacle Island, Boston Harbor, Boston

Wallace Floyd Associates; Brown and Rowe

Spectacle Island is a sanitary landfill that incorporates millions of cubic yards of dredged fill from the Central Artery/Third Harbor Tunnel excavation. Brown and Rowe's plan calls for thousands of trees and shrubs to be planted in three to five feet of topsoil, thus stabilizing the fill underneath. To avoid stripping local topsoil for the project, Brown and Rowe worked with soil scientist Dr. Phillip Craul to develop a manufactured topsoil including glacial till, sand, and recycled organic matter. Native plants such as sumac, blueberries, viburnums, and clematis help to control erosion. Grasses and wildflowers will cover the southern slope, evergreens will create windbreaks, and plants attractive to birds will promote future self-seeding.

Wallace Floyd has planned for the visitors' center at the intersection of the island's marina, a seaside promenade, and hillside paths. Public art created from materials washed up on its beaches may be included as wall mosaics in the visitors' center, reflecting the island's past as a landfill site.

Carol R. Johnson Associates is providing final landscape design for Deer Island, the site of the new secondary wastewater treatment facility in Boston Harbor. The landscape design includes the planting of grass, shrubs, and trees that are indigenous to the harbor islands—vegetation capable of thriving in the harsh island environment. The design serves several purposes: earth stabilization, revegetation, the fostering of coastal wildlife, the accentuating of landform design, and vegetative screening. These design features will help to link Deer Island more closely as a recreational and open space resource with the other islands in the Boston Harbor Island chain.

Carol R. Johnson Associates designed the primary and secondary trail systems and interpretive signage on the island. The primary trail will provide access all around the island and will be handicapped accessible, and both trail systems will support emergency vehicles such as ambulances. Signs will give visitors a general orientation, as well as discuss historic and interpretive elements.

Deer Island Wastewater Treatment Facility MWRA (133)

Deer Island Boston Harbor, Boston

Carol R. Johnson Associates

World's End comprises 251 acres on two coastal drumlins extending into the southern edge of Boston Harbor. The late 1880s master plan by Frederick Law Olmsted Sr. depicted a residential subdivision that was never built. The carriage paths, however, were laid out and planted generally according to Olmsted's plan. Today the landscape at World's End reveals Olmsted's vision for this unbuilt residential community. It features romantic curvilinear paths, mature tree plantings, meadows, rocky shores, marshes, and spectacular hilltop views of the harbor and downtown Boston. World's End is owned and managed by the Trustees of Reservations and is now part of the Boston Harbor Islands Partnership.

World's End (134)

Martin's Lane, Hingham

Frederick Law Olmsted Sr.

This Metropolitan District Commission Park is part of the Neponset River Master Plan. The park, scheduled for completion in the fall of 2000, will include a multipurpose field, a parking lot, a children's playground, passive areas with extensive plantings of native species, over two miles of walking and jogging paths, and community gardens. This park will be built on two sites, one, a former landfill, and the other, the former site of a drive-in movie theater. Innovative construction procedures were used to reduce costs and speed up construction. Large quantities of debris were moved between the sites to make them comply with environmental and regulatory guidelines and to provide visually interesting landforms. In addition, two acres of salt marsh will be created along this tidal section of the Neponset River.

Pope John Paul II Park (135)

Neponset River at Southeast Expressway off Gallivan Road, Boston

Camp Dresser and McKee in collaboration with Pressley Associates

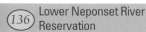

(136) Lower Neponset River Reservation

Boston

Metropolitan District Commission

The Lower Neponset River Reservation, part of the Boston Metropolitan Park System, is rich in natural and cultural resources. It provides a home to many species of fish and wildlife and has a long and varied history of human uses. Recent master planning identified various goals for landscape design: preserving the natural qualities of the river system, increasing public access and recreational opportunities, and educating users about the history and culture of the river and surrounding areas. Specific plans include the creation of pedestrian trails throughout the park, interpretive displays of the river's ecology, community gardens, and a canoe launch.

(137) Boston College, Campus Entrance

Commonwealth Avenue, Chestnut Hill, Boston

Sasaki Associates

Boston College's new main entrance off Commonwealth Avenue unifies and defines the edge of the campus thereby creating a stronger sense of identity for the college. It also provides greater safety for pedestrians and automobiles and a more coherent orientation for visitors. An arrangement of stone piers, a new guard booth, metal fencing, identification signage, and plantings complement rows of old linden trees that line the drive.

(138) Blue Hills Reservation

Hillside Street, Milton

Charles Eliot, Metropolitan District Commission

This enormous woodland reservation of nearly 6,000 acres contains many varieties of trees, shrubs and wildflowers which provide a habitat for several rare or endangered wildlife species, including the Timber Rattlesnake. As well the reservation contains over 50 prehistoric sites, 16 historic structures listed on the National Register, three National Environmental Study Areas, the Blue Hills Meteorological Observatory, the Trailside Museum, and the Ponkapoag Golf Course. The reservation also contains several hilltops ranging from 300 to 635 feet, including Great Blue Hill. The highest point along the Atlantic Coast south of Maine, Great Blue Hill provides a location for downhill skiing close to the city.

Operated by the National Park Service as a National Historic Site, this property has been preserved to reflect the four generations of the Adams family who lived here from 1787 to 1927, including Presidents John Adams and John Quincy Adams. The site contains the Old House, several outbuildings, a museum collection, formal gardens, and a duck pond. Not only does the site teach about the politically and socially important Adams family, but because it was owned by one family for so long, it also reveals historical trends in land use and landscape design over a 150 year period.

Adams National Historic Site

Quincy
USDA National Park Service

Marina Bay on Boston Harbor is a four-hundred-acre mixed-use residential and commercial development focusing on a revitalized marina for up to six hundred vessels. The site includes shops, condominiums, offices, restaurants, assisted living, and nursing home facilities. The designers have unified the area by standardizing the details for plantings and lighting, as well as for and pedestrian and vehicular circulation systems throughout the complex. Special features include a black-bottom reflecting pool, modern sculpture by artist Obie Simonis, a 1500' waterfront boardwalk, and roof deck gardens with beautiful harbor views.

Marina Bay

Victory Road, Squantum
Mary Smith Associates

Constitution Common is an entry plaza and public garden between City Hall and Hancock Street, adjacent to the local MBTA subway stop. It introduces visitors to the city of Quincy with an arcade of cherry trees. It includes a central octagonal planting bed surrounded by benches, large areas of lawn, stately trees, and flower beds. Donors names are inscribed on over five thousand paving bricks, instilling a sense of pride in both the project and the city.

Constitution Common & Quincy City Hall

1305 Hancock Street, Quincy
Mary Smith Associates

(142) The Eleanor Cabot Bradley Reservation

2468B Washington Street, Canton

Charles A. Platt

Designed in 1902, this property features a Georgian-style house and formal gardens with excellent views of the surrounding Blue Hills. More distant parts of the property contain paths winding through hay fields, pasture land, quiet woods, and—a pleasant surprise to hikers—artfully hidden ponds. The working parts of the estate include a walled garden, small orchard, greenhouse, and sunken camellia house, all still in use.

(143) The Hunnewell Estate

845 Washington Street, Wellesley

Hunnewell Family

Originally called Wellesley, this estate has been in the same family for 150 years. Horatio Hunnewell, the first resident, created a formal Italian garden for the steep site with a style unique to the time, featuring terraces and geometrical topiary forms. An avid collector of plants from all over the world, Hunnewell developed the site's pinetum, which today contains some of the oldest rare pines in the country. The estate also contains an extensive rhododendron collection.

(144) Elmbank

900 Washington Street (Route 16), Wellesley

Olmsted Brothers; Pressley Associates

This estate, planned around the turn of the century, featured Victorian garden beds, English woods for carriage rides, and elm tree plantings inspired by those along the Charles River in the 18th century. The Olmsted brothers later designed some of the grounds, including an Italianate Garden and an Oriental Garden with a Japanese bridge, a pond, and a temple. In addition, there is also a greenhouse, a wetlands vernal pool, and trial seed gardens. The Italianate garden is currently under restoration. The site is jointly owned by the Metropolitan District Commission and the Massachusetts Horticultural Society.

The 1997 master plan for the upper section of the Charles River reservation, "the forgotten Charles," restores the riverfront and provides continuous public access along a five-and-three-quarter mile section of the river from Watertown Square to Route 128 in Weston. This historically industrial section of the river has suffered a century of abuse and neglect, which is only now being addressed. With both an ecological and cultural inter-

(145) Upper Charles River Master Plan and Phased Implementation

Watertown, Newton, Waltham, and Weston

Carol R. Johnson Associates

pretation of the river's industrial heritage, the plan marks trail routes and access points through a complex and ecologically diverse urban landscape. In this on-going project, the builders have worked to mitigate the impact of trail construction through the use of innovative building practices and materials. Extensive plantings of native species are helping to restore the ecological health of the corridor.

This parcel of land owned by the Church of Jesus Christ of Latter-day Saints was developed to include a church and parking facility as well as twenty-two marketable single family homes. Spectacular natural features of the property were preserved including steep slopes, fractured stone outcroppings, ledges, and mature stands of oaks. The project received a BSLA Honor Award for Institutional Landscapes in 1986.

Church of Jesus Christ of Latter-day Saints (146)
15 Ledgewood Place, Belmont
Carol R. Johnson Associates

Established in 1893 as the first acquisition of the Metropolitan Parks Commission, Beaver Brook Reservation is 65 acres of open fields, wetlands, and woodlands. The less developed northern section of the park contains ponds and a cascading waterfall, creating a memorable setting for walking and picnicking. The more developed southern section contains ballfields, a wading pool, and a tot lot. Also on the grounds are the Robert Morris Copeland House (c. 1835), and a monument to the Waverly Oaks, an ancient grove of White Oak trees that have all since succumbed to old age. Since its establishment the reservation has been renovated in 1960 By Shurcliff and Merrill, and in 1990 by The Halvorson Company.

Beaver Brook Reservation (147)
Mill Street, Belmont/Waltham
Charles Eliot, Shurcliff and Merrill; The Halvorson Company; Metropolitan District Commission

Danehy Park is the first park in the Boston region to be built on a former landfill. The fifty-acre park opened in 1990 and provides extensive recreational facilities. It has football, soccer, and softball fields; two-and-a-half miles of pathways for walking and jogging; public art; an artificial wetland for storm-water management and nature study; picnic areas; toddler playgrounds; a spray pool; an amphitheater; and parking places for over three hundred vehicles. Danehy Park is one of Cambridge's most valuable recreational resources, providing 20 percent of the city's open space. The park has been recognized by many as an innovative reuse of a former landfill.

Danehy Park (148)
Sherman/New Streets Cambridge
Camp Dresser and McKee with Moriece and Gary

Jefferson Park, built in the 1950s, was a dormitory-style housing project set in a sea of asphalt. By the early 1980's it no longer met the needs of its tenants. Its redesign decreased the total number of units and provided each one with a backyard to encourage ownership and maintenance responsibility. Former asphalt-covered areas now contain attractive planted playgrounds, and earthen berms buffer the noise from adjacent commuter rail lines. In 1985 this project won an Honor Award for Multi-Family Housing from the BSLA.

Jefferson Park (149)
Between Rindge Avenue and the Railroad Corridor, next to Catholic Cemetery, Cambridge
The SWA Group

<table>
<tr><td>

(150) **Porter Square
MBTA Station**

Cambridge

Carol R. Johnson Associates

</td><td>

Commuter rail lines, the MBTA's Red Line subway, and bus routes converge at this busy transit station. Features such as bicycle storage, comfortable seating, and bronze and stone sculptures by artist David Phillips make the commute through Porter Square memorable and enjoyable. Six different artists were commissioned to create art works for the site, and Carol R. Johnson Associates worked with artists in planning how their works would be incorporated into the site.

</td></tr>
</table>

(151) Arsenal Park

Arsenal Street, Watertown

John Wacker and Associates

This fourteen-acre multi-use park is located on the site of a former military arsenal. Designed to appeal to people of all ages, the park has undeveloped open space, mature trees, children's play areas, an amphitheater, and a physical fitness course. Concrete foundation slabs from demolished arsenal buildings now provide hard surface play areas for activities like tennis and basketball. The military parade ground is now an open lawn play area. The park received a BSLA Merit Award in 1986.

(152) Lyman Estate, The Vale

185 Lyman Street , Waltham

Theodore Lyman

Begun in 1793, the Lyman Estate was one of the first in the area to be laid out in the English landscape style. The grounds include a dammed brook forming a small lake, and a brick wall which screens the kitchen garden and farmyard from the house and provides protection and warmth for espaliered fruit trees. Beautiful mature trees cover the landscape, some standing alone as magnificent specimens, others planted in informal clusters. Today the property is owned by the Society for the Preservation of New England Antiquities and is open to the public. The estate contains the main house, restored gardens, and greenhouses that hold a tremendous collection of exotic plants.

This beautiful 250-acre park is the oldest and largest public open space in Waltham, but it has slowly deteriorated over the years. Recent master planning for the park, which won a BSLA Merit Award in 1997, includes a ten phase program which will increase opportunities for passive recreation and improve pedestrian accessibility, especially up to the summit of Big and Little Prospect Hills. As the second highest point in the metropolitan area the park offers unparalleled views of Boston. Ultimately the goal is to return this park to its former status as a source of pride and a focal point for the surrounding community.

Prospect Hill Park (153)
Totten Pond Road, Waltham
Walker-Kluesing Design Group

Steep topography and environmental constraints made this beautiful fifty-eight-acre site a challenge to develop. The solution involved planted terraces organized around atria and connected by an internal "street." Building groups set within this terraced landscape are oriented in various directions, each one enjoying a different view. Depending on location, one can see the Cambridge Reservoir, the Boston skyline, or the nearby woodlands.

Bay Colony Corporate Center (154)
Waltham
Sasaki Associates

Walter Gropius, founder of the German design school Bauhaus, built this home for himself when he came to teach at Harvard's Graduate School of Design. Modestly sized, the house combines traditional elements of New England architecture with innovative materials, creating a revolutionary and influential design. The house and landscape—the site of a former orchard—are well integrated. Both were planned for maximum efficiency and simplicity. The property now belongs to the Society for the Preservation of New England Antiquities and is open to visitors as a house museum with the family's possessions still in place. (Call for visits: 617-259-8843.)

Gropius House (155)
68 Baker Bridge Road, Lincoln
Walter Gropius with
Marcel Breuer

(156) The Codman House

Codman Road, Lincoln

Codman Family

Once part of a 450-acre estate belonging to the Codman family, the house and 16 acres of the grounds now belong to the Society for the Preservation of New England Antiquities. It is open to the public as a museum and a location for special events. The landscape design done by the many generations of Codmans who lived here reflects national trends: in the early 1800s, for instance, they practiced experimental horticulture with varieties of plant species, and around the turn of the century they planted an Italianate garden. Ogden Codman Jr., co-author of the book "The Decoration of Houses" with Edith Wharton, is thought to have designed the Italian garden.

(157) Walden Pond State Reservation

Route 126 at Route 2, Concord

Walker-Kluesing Design Group

Made famous in the writings of Henry David Thoreau, Walden Pond and the landscape around it are an internationally known symbol for man living in harmony with nature. Recently the north and south shorelines of this national historic landmark were restored to a more natural, stable condition in a process that eliminated years of damage from heavy recreational use. A pedestrian path follows the perimeter of the pond and provides handicapped access from Red Cross Beach to the Thoreau house site. The path materials were selected to blend with the natural surroundings and resist erosion, and new plantings are ecologically appropriate and historically accurate, following

the descriptions given in Thoreau's writings. Soil erosion was reduced through the use of conventional practices as well as bioengineering techniques.

Consecrated in 1855, Sleepy Hollow Cemetery exemplifies the nine-teenth-century "rural cemetery" style. In their design, Horace W. S. Cleveland and Robert Morris Copeland, who were inspired by the writings of romanticists Ralph Waldo Emerson, Nathaniel Hawthorne, and Henry David Thoreau, incorporated native woodlands, steep slopes, and a bowl-shaped glen. In 1908, sculptor and landscape designer Daniel Chester French added a monument dedicated to three brothers killed in the Civil War: "Mourning Victory" typifies French's style, with evergreens serving as a dark background to the pink marble sculpture. A recent rehabilitation plan, completed by Denig Design Associates and landscape historian Sarah Collins la Cour, recommends restoring a pond, replanting native woodlands, and reconstructing the landscape around "Mourning Victory."

Sleepy Hollow Cemetery (158)

Bedford Street, Concord

Horace W. S. Cleveland and Robert Morris Copeland; Daniel Chester French;

Denig Design Associates; Sarah Collins la Cour

Minute Man National Historical Park and Battle Road Trail

(159)

Monument Street and Route 2A, Concord, Lincoln and Lexington

National Park Service, Carol R. Johnson Associates

This historic park features the Old North Bridge, the site of "the shot heard 'round the world," the first real battle of the American Revolution on April 19, 1775. The bridge is set in an open landscape managed by the National Park Service to reflect the Colonial appearance of 1775. This landscape has been partially restored to its Colonial character. A new four-and-a-half-mile trail provides visitors with safe access to a formerly inaccessible area containing various historic sites. The trail follows the battle route taken by the retreating British forces and their Colonial pursuers after the battle. The trail winds through farmlands, forests, and wetlands, allowing visitors to experience both natural and cultural features. The trail's impact on environmentally sensitive areas was minimized through careful routing and building methods. The construction of animal underpasses was given special consideration— for example, the structures were made from recycled plastic, a chemically inert material that will not affect groundwater.

The Minute Man Bikeway

(160)

Arlington, Lexington, and Bedford

CityDesign Collaborative

The Minuteman Bikeway is an alternative transportation corridor connecting several outlying towns to the MBTA subway system. During the proposal stage, abutters and other interested parties voiced concerns through public and individual meetings, the result of which was a design that incorporated plantings and fences for privacy and security. Artists on the design team helped to create thematic bollards, missile barriers, mile markers, gates, and signage. In 1994 this project received a BSLA Award for Parks and Recreation.

Arlington Memorial Park

(161)

Massachusetts Avenue, Arlington

Sasaki Associates

This one-half-acre park commemorates several treasured elements of the town of Arlington's history, from its colonial township days to its later incarnation as a streetcar suburb. Two parlor gardens and a historic fence surround a nineteenth-century house—the 1832 Jefferson Cutter home. Arlington's first railroad station sat on the park's premises and is marked by the historic railroad bed that now runs through its center. The park lies among a cluster of prominent homes surrounding a town common that still retains its old character. In 1990, it received a Merit Award from the BSLA for park and recreation design.

Prior to 1963 this church was surrounded by blacktop. Leaders wanted to improve its appearance to reflect the dignity of the church as well as to contribute to the improvement of Main Street. Shade trees now frame the church and continue out to the street in a welcoming manner. Strips of brick over the exposed aggregate further connect the church and the street, while flowering trees and shrubs add variety and seasonal change. In 1986 this project received a BSLA Award for Mature Projects.

This 2,075 acre reservation of rocky, hilly terrain provides visitors with opportunities for hiking, horseback riding, rock climbing, mountain biking, and cross-country skiing. Rich in history, the park offers educational programs that teach visitors about its past, during periods when it was a source of timber, granite, ice, and water power. Bellevue Pond, located within the park, is surrounded by trails leading to Wrights Tower, which provides a fine view of the Boston Basin.

This 180-acre park is an excellent example of the reclamation of a former dump site. It won an Honor Award from the ASLA in 1982 and a Governor's Design Award in 1986. The park incorporates a network of pathways, vegetation, and modest hillocks along the Mystic River waterfront. Future pedestrian pathways and bikeways will connect the park with public transportation and provide increased accessibility. The park serves adjacent new neighborhoods as well as older ones farther away.

Bendetson Hall on the main green of Tufts University was recently renovated as the new Admissions Center. A formal brick forecourt, arranged around two magnificent cherry trees, welcomes visitors outside the main entrance and provides a place to gather. Reconfigured walkways direct visitors to the Admissions Center from the main green. A terrace added to the back of the building provides a place for staff to eat lunch and take breaks. In 1988 this project received a BSLA Merit Award for Institutional Design.

Located on a sloping site, Tufts University's Mayer Campus Center connects the residential facilities located below it with the academic buildings further up the hill. The main entrance is directly across the street from a relocated gate leading to the central academic part of campus; this orientation makes the Campus Center a key pedestrian link between two otherwise separated areas. The landscape design reflects the building's prairie-style architecture in its use of terraces, walls, steps, and bollards, creating a unity of site and building. In 1987 this project won a Merit Award for Institutional Design from the BSLA.

(167) Tufts University, Tisch Family Library

Medford

Walker-Kluesing Design Group

This library was recently renovated, adding 80,000 square feet of new space and partially remodeling the existing structure. Because of the sloping site, the incorporation of handicapped access was a particular challenge. This was met by carefully integrating steps and ramps and sensitive grading to reduce handrail requirements. The newly designed entryway features attractive granite paving, plantings, bicycle parking, and a small bronze sculpture of Barnum and Bailey's "Jumbo the Elephant" which was moved to become a focal point in the entrance courtyard.

(168) Woodstock and Osgood Parks

Woodstock Street and Alewife Brook Parkway; Osgood Street, Somerville

Wallace Floyd Associates

Woodstock and Osgood are neighborhood parks which include playgrounds, spray pools, picnic areas, basketball courts, and community gardens. The Woodstock Park reflects the history of the area thematically through trolley-based designs, while the Osgood Park presents a different history through an orchard motif. The themes give each park its own identity and are a playful way of introducing neighborhood history and character.

(169) Davis Square and MBTA Station

Davis Square, College Avenue, Somerville

Childs, Bertman, Tseckares and Casendino

Carol R. Johnson Associates

Redesigned as part of the subway Red Line extension project, this square consists of historic nineteenth-century elements such as brick sidewalks, acorn-style lighting, benches, and tree plantings. These features blend this modern amenity with the older surrounding neighborhood. A raised granite and bronze compass located in the square commemorates the founding of Somerville in 1883. In reorganizing the square's traffic pattern, care was taken to increase pedestrian safety.

Carol R. Johnson Associates designed the new MBTA station site, which includes two head houses and an interconnecting plaza. The site also contains a public busway with planted walkways on either side. Community input during the development process contributed to the final designs for plantings, brick and granite paving, and lighting. The plaza also includes game tables and benches that contribute to commuters' enjoyment and comfort. In 1988 this project received a BSLA Honor Award for Urban Design.

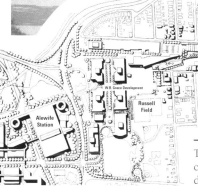

This one-mile linear park is constructed on an abandoned railroad right-of-way above a new subway tunnel. In addition to providing the neighborhood with a pedestrian and bike path that links two subway stations on the MBTA's Red Line, the project also helped to revitalize two local business districts. The design allows neighborhood residents to enjoy views into the park without losing their privacy, and public safety is preserved through careful pathway alignment, earthwork design, planting, and lighting. The project won awards from the Massachusetts Horticultural Society, the BSLA, and the Governor's Design Award Program.

Davis Square to Alewife Linear Park

Davis Square, behind the MBTA Station (Somerville), Massachusetts Avenue and Harvey Street (Cambridge), Somerville and Cambridge

Wallace Floyd Associates

During the early 1990s this forty-year-old public housing development was renovated and won a BSLA Award for Housing Design. New streets were constructed within the development, and front entrances were reoriented to face the streets. Each main entrance now opens onto a semi-public courtyard, providing individual front yard space. The raised site provides barrier-free access to building entryways.

The Mystics (171)

30 Memorial Road, Somerville

Weinmayr Associates

This small park sits in a dense urban area and serves as both playground and social focus for the neighborhood. A centrally located fountain provides a place for water play, and its innovative design of sprayers located at pavement level prevents vandalism. When the fountain is turned off, the area becomes an open plaza for special events, festivals, and gatherings. The park also contains playground and picnic facilities.

Bosson Park (172)

Bellingham/Grove Streets, Chelsea

Francis Fox Spinks Associates

This school's location along the Chelsea River inspired an innovative interpretive design. The Waterfront Park Playground imaginatively recreates Boston Harbor in miniature, complete with a water spray for the summer. A large world map on one half of the playground, which also serves as a spray pool, illustrates the historic importance of Boston Harbor and aids students in visualizing the geographic relationships between Chelsea and places from which they or their ancestors may have immigrated. This design won a BSLA Merit Award in 1997.

Mary C. Burke Elementary School

300 Crescent Avenue, Chelsea

Carol R. Johnson Associates

(174) Revere Beach Reservation and Master Plan Revere Charles Eliot; Metropolitan District Commission (MDC); Carol R. Johnson Associates	Located on the ocean shore north of Boston, Revere Beach was the first public beach secured under the Metropolitan Plan by Charles Eliot in 1893. Eliot found the condition of the beach a "disgrace" and developed a plan to remove an existing railroad and housing to accommodate public use. Managed by the MDC, the beach has been intensively used ever since, According to the master plan by Carol R. Johnson and Associates, Revere Beach Reservation will include approximately three miles of ocean beach and twenty-five acres of adjoining parkland. The character of the new Reservation will be as natural as possible with an emphasis on densely planted indigenous vegetation, ocean views, and passive recreation. Site improvements for the linear park include winding paths for biking, walking, and jogging, benches, lighting, and play areas, and restoration of the historic beach pavilions.
(175) Saugus Iron Works 244 Central Street, Saugus National Park Service	Developed in 1646-48, this National Historic Site was the first integrated ironworks in North America. It trained skilled iron workers for what would become America's iron and steel industry, and therefore played a vital role in shaping the early history of our nation. Operated today as an open-air museum, the site contains the archeological site of the 17th century iron-making plant, a museum collection, and the reconstructed iron works complex, all providing visitors with a unique experience of this important historic resource.
(176) High Rock Essex Street, Lynn Frederick Law Olmsted Sr.; Walker-Kluesing Design Group	This romantic park, with splendid views of the city and ocean, will soon be rehabilitated under the Massachusetts Department of Environmental Management's Olmsted Historic Landscape Preservation Program. Its dramatic sloping site and rock outcrops will be accentuated by removing overgrowth, and walks, steps, and walls will incorporate site materials. Plans also include the restoration of a stone cottage in the park which will contain interpretive features explaining the history of this traditional community meeting place. The park has been expanded to the south, incorporating a large underused traffic island.

Map 4 – Boston-North Shore

177. Downtown Salem, Heritage Plaza East/West
178. Pickering Wharf, Salem
179. House of the Seven Gables Historic Site,
    Salem
180. Salem Witch Trials Tercentenary Memorial
181. Riley Plaza, Salem
182. Salem Common
183. The Sedgewick Gardens at Long Hill, Beverly
184. Moraine Farm, Beverly
185. Coolidge Reservation, Manchester
186. Stacy Waterfront Park, Gloucester
187. Ravenswood Park, Gloucester
188. Halibut Point, Rockport
189. Castle Hill, the Crane Estate, Ipswich
190. John Whipple House, Ipswich

191. Market Landing Park, Newburypport
192. Maudslay State Park Master Plan,
    Newburyport
193. Newburyport Waterfront and Business
    District Improvements

(above) Stacey Park, Gloucester; (below) Salem Common;
(background) the Crane Estate

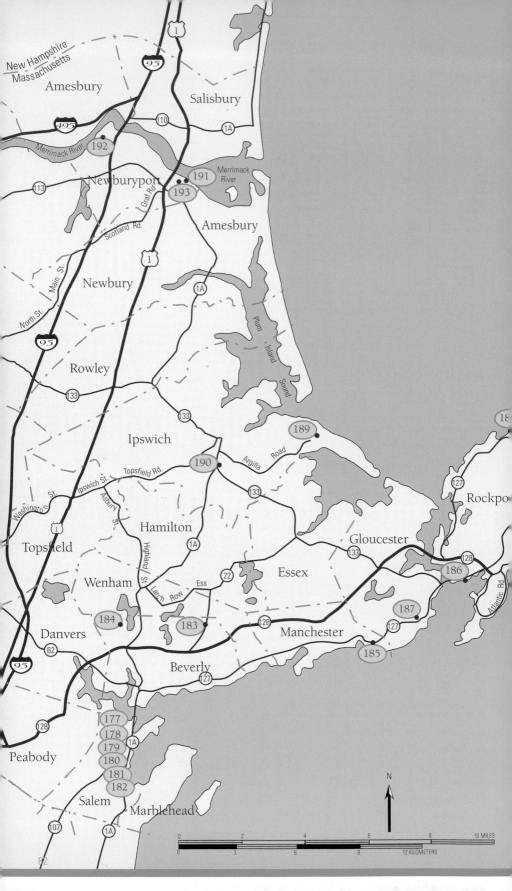

North Shore

Several city blocks were redeveloped during the reclamation of historic downtown Salem, reviving the local economy by increasing tourism and private development. Key buildings were linked to each other by courts, plazas, and pedestrian malls. An old parking lot in front of city hall was transformed into a mini plaza and amphitheater for public events. The use of granite and brick and the placement of street trees provide a sense of unity and completeness. The project received an ASLA honor award in 1983.

Downtown Salem, Heritage Plaza East/West (177)

Salem

The Delta Group

Pickering Wharf is an important historical resource on the Salem waterfront. During the colonial period, ships sailed the world from this location. In later years the wharf fell into decline, becoming first a coal yard, then an oil tank farm. Following revitalization, the area now includes housing and retail shops that recall a historic waterfront village, and it is within walking distance of other historic sites in Salem, including the House of the Seven Gables. Concept drawings for this project received a Progressive Architecture Award, and the completed project received an excellence award in architecture from the Boston Society of Architects.

Pickering Wharf (178)

Salem Waterfront , Salem

Pressley Associates

One of the oldest surviving 17th century wooden mansions in New England, this historic house served as the setting for Nathaniel Hawthorn's classic novel of the same name. It is open to the public as a museum, and is part of a larger Historic Site which includes an 18th century granite sea wall, the original location of Captain John Turner's wharf, and two seaside Colonial Revival gardens. The museum contains information about Nathaniel Hawthorn, as well as about William Sumner Appleton, an active local preservationist and founder of the Society for the Preservation of New England Antiquities (SPNEA).

House of the Seven Gables Historic Site (179)

54 Turner Street, Salem

This memorial, remembering twenty innocent people who were put to death as witches in Salem in 1692, consists of a low granite wall supporting twenty cantilevered benches. The wall and benches surround a grassy courtyard planted with black locust trees. Each bench is dedicated to one victim and contains the person's name, date, and manner of execution. The use of granite and black locust trees have symbolic

Salem Witch Trials Tercentenary Memorial (180)

Adjacent to Charter Street Burial Ground, Salem

James Cutler Architects;
Maggie Smith, Sculptor;
The Halvorson Company

meaning as both were used in the executions. A stone entryway is etched with the words of the victims protesting their innocence. Winner of the 1996 BSLA Honor Award for Landscape Art and Earth Sculpture, this design illustrates the power of landscape to elicit a strong emotional response.

(181) Riley Plaza

Washington and New Derby Street, Salem

Wallace Floyd Associates

The complete redesign of Riley Plaza included the reconfiguration of roadways and parking lots to improve safety and define the plaza as a gateway to the city of Salem. The plaza is a major entry point to the central business district and several of the city's tourist attractions. It includes custom granite seating focused toward a circle of ship's flags which celebrate the city's maritime history.

(182) Salem Common

Washington Square, Salem

Wallace Floyd Associates

Salem Common is a nine-acre park located in the heart of downtown Salem and is surrounded by handsome federal-style homes. The design sought to return the park to its original 1850s appearance through the restoration of a cast-iron fence that defines the perimeter, realignment of the path system, and restoration of an historic bandstand for concerts and other activities. In 1990 the project won the Massachusetts Horticultural Society Citation for Historic Restoration.

(183) The Sedgewick Gardens at Long Hill

572 Essex Street, Beverly

Mabel Cabot Sedgewick;
Marjorie Russell Sedgewick

Long Hill is now headquarters of the Trustees of Reservations, a statewide nonprofit conservation organization, but it began as an early-twentieth-century "Country Place" estate. The site consists of a summer house built in 1916 by *Atlantic Monthly* magazine editor Ellery Sedgewick. Sedgewick and his wife built the house in the southern antebellum style using salvaged, ornately carved woodwork from the early-nineteenth-century Ball Home in Charleston, South Carolina. The house is nestled in among 114 acres of designed gardens and natural woodlands. Paths wind through acres of gardens, which range from English to Japanese in character. There are over four hundred species of plants, including many rare varieties selected in collaboration with the Arnold Arboretum. Foot trails also traverse the flora- and fauna-filled woodlands.

Frederick Law Olmsted Sr.'s 1880 design for this private estate aimed to serve both the interests of his client, John Phillips, and those of the burgeoning scientific community. It has been labeled "the finest example of Olmsted's approach to planning a country estate." His intentions for the 275-acre landscape are still very much alive: it is a country retreat in the eighteenth-century English landscape tradition, with rolling pastures and framed vistas. At the same time, it is a laboratory for scientific farming and experimental forestry. Project Adventure Inc, a leader in experienced based training and development, has its international headquarters at Moraine Farm. Call John Little of Project Adventure to arrange visits at 978-524-4659.

The Moraine Farm (184)
719 Cabot Street, Beverly
Frederick Law Olmsted Sr.

The Coolidge Reservation, owned and managed by The Trustees for Reservations, is located on a scenic peninsula east of the village of Manchester. The spectacular site consists of a rocky headland, the expansive Ocean Lawn with magnificent specimen trees and panoramic views of the ocean, mature woodlands, massive ledges, a tidal stream, a scenic freshwater pond, and a stretch of Magnolia beach. CRJA prepared a master plan to provide for public passive recreation while ensuring the scenic and environmental values of this unique property.

Coolidge Reservation (185)
Manchester
Carol R. Johnson Associates

Stacy Boulevard Waterfront Park is a national monument dedicated to those lost at sea. Its exposed location on a broad sweep of land overlooking Gloucester Harbor provides visitors with spectacular views of the Atlantic Ocean. Restoration included rebuilding the seawall to minimize storm damage due to the harsh marine conditions; in addition, pedestrian pathways throughout the park, decorative lighting, and historical sign posting have created a lasting, comfortable, and engaging place to visit.

Stacy Waterfront Park (186)
Gloucester
John Copley and Associates

(187) Ravenswood Park

Western Avenue (Route 127),
Gloucester

Samuel Sawyer and the
Trustees of Reservations

This beautiful 550-acre park, owned and managed by the Trustees of Reservations, contains woodlands preserved in their natural state. There are three miles of carriage roads and seven miles of trails, some winding past glacial erratics (boulders) and some offering views of Gloucester harbor. On this site in 1806, Theophilus Parsons discovered the Sweetbay magnolia, *Magnolia virginiana*. The tree was much sought after and almost became extinct from overcollection, but through replanting and careful conservation the stewards of Ravenswood saved the park's collection.

(188) Halibut Point

Gott Avenue, Rockport

The Trustees of Reservations

Jointly owned and managed by the Trustees of Reservations and the Massachusetts Department of Environmental Management, this spectacular landscape has been preserved for public enjoyment. The Point features panoramic views of surf and distant lands, as well as a diverse landscape including tidal pools, heathlands, scrub forests, and ledges. Standing on the rocky headlands of Cape Ann is a fifty-foot-tall grout pile known as "The Halibut," which has been a regional landmark for centuries. Halibut Point was the site of a major granite quarry during the late nineteenth and early twentieth centuries.

Designed for the Crane family in the early 1900s, the development of this seaside property is a good example of the large-scale residential planning that characterized the Country Place Era, a period in America during which rural tracts of land were transformed into refined estates. Olmsted Brothers completed much of the landscape design for the site, including a formal Italian garden; in addition, Crane and Arthur Shurcliff designed a hedge maze, and Shurcliff alone did much later work, such as a grand allée placing the rear façade of the house on axis with a clear and spectacular view of the

(189) Castle Hill, The Crane Estate

Argilla Road, Ipswich

Olmsted Brothers; Arthur
Shurcliff; Ernest Bowditch

Atlantic. Unfortunately, today most of the gardens are no longer in cultivation and the hedge maze no longer exists.

Adjacent to Castle Hill lies the two-thousand-acre Crane Beach and Crane Wildlife Refuge, with a salt marsh, an estuary, islands, dunes, a maritime forest, and miles of unspoiled barrier beach. The beach contains a dune boardwalk system which successfully allows the dynamic dune processes of erosion and deposition to continue while still providing beach access. The Crane Estate is owned and managed by the Trustees of Reservations.

This 1655 colonial-style house was moved to its current location in the twentieth century. Historical research suggests that John Whipple coordinated with J. Winthrop in establishing gardens on the original site, and Ann Leighton has reconstructed an amalgamation of gardens, accurately reproducing colonial-period forms and plant selections, including crushed clamshell paths.

John Whipple House and Herb Garden
190

Route 1A, Ipswich
Ann Leighton

This waterfront park in the historic north shore town of Newburyport is a simple yet elegant space for passive recreation and civic events. It links the downtown and waterfront with several pedestrian pathways, drawing visitors into the park. A granite balustrade and stage platform provides a beautiful setting for special events, and broad open lawns offer panoramic harbor views. Design details within the park are in keeping with the district's federalist architecture and add to the character and charm of this historic town. The project received a Merit Award from the BSLA in 1988.

Market Landing Park
191

Merrimack Street
Newburyport
The Halvorson Company

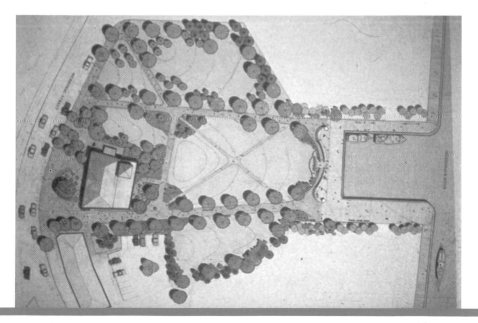

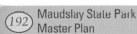
In 1985 the state of Massachusetts purchased the 450-acre Maudslay Estate, adapting it for use as a park. Master planning included partial restoration of the original formal gardens designed by Martha Brooks Hutcheson, one of the first female members of the ASLA. It also included the creation of an historic landscape sequence that brings visitors through the original main gates, the restored formal gardens, and a greenhouse complex. The site's gently rolling hills and open fields contain a unique collection of specimen trees, as well as a bald eagle roosting area. In 1988 the project received a BSLA Honor Award for Landscape Planning.

Sasaki Associates redesigned this historic seaport waterfront and business district to revitalize the local economy and improve environmental and structural problems. The renovated waterfront, which now includes a boardwalk, has encouraged private development of parcels immediately inland. In addition, renovations to the business district—a fountain, plazas, and walkways that use traditional materials—followed guidelines developed to preserve the historic character of the city.

References and Additional Information

Institutions, Libraries and Archives:

**The Frederick Law Olmsted
National Historic Site**
An historical archives for Olmsted research.
99 Warren Street, Brookline, MA. 02146
(617) 566-1689,
Open Friday, Saturday and Sunday,
10:00 AM to 4:30 PM, or by appointment.

**The Loeb Library of the
Harvard Graduate School of Design**
Harvard University
Quincy Street, Cambridge, MA.

**Wave Hill,
The Catalog of Landscape Documents**
675 West 252nd Street
Bronx, NY 10471 (718) 549-3200

Boston Atheneum
(617) 227-0270

Schlinger Library at Radcliffe

The Boston Public Library
Boylston Street
Boston, MA

Boston Parks and Recreation Department
1010 Massachusetts Avenue
Boston, MA 02118
(617) 635-4505

**The Metropolitan District Commission
Archives**
20 Somerset Street
Boston, MA 02108

The Trustees of Reservations
572 Essex Street, Beverly , MA.01915
(508) 921-1944

**The U.S. Department of Interior, National
Park Service.**
15 State Street
Boston, MA 02109
(617) 223-5042

National Association for Olmsted Parks
7315 Wisconsin Avenue, Room 705 East
Bethesda, MD 20814

**Society for the Preservation of New England
Antiquities (SPNEA)**
141 Cambridge Street
Boston, MA 02114
(617) 227-3956

Books and Publications:

Garden of Memories: A Guide to Historic Forest Hills. Susan Wilson, Forest Hills Educational Trust, 1998. 144 pp.

Fairsted: A Cultural Landscape Report for the Frederick Law Olmsted National Historic Site. Volume 1: Site History. Cynthia Zaitzevsky. Olmsted Center for Landscape Preservation, National Park Service, and the Arnold Arboretum of Harvard University. 1997. 253 pp.

Silent City on a Hill: Landscapes of Memory and Boston's Mount Auburn Cemetery. Blanche Linden-Ward. Ohio State University Press, Columbus. 1989. 403 pp.

Boston's Changeful Times: Origins of Preservation and Planning in America. Michael Holleran. Johns Hopkins University Press, Baltimore. 1998. 337 pp.

Science in the Pleasure Ground: A History of the Arnold Arboretum. Ida Hay. 1995.

Frederick Law Olmsted and the Boston Park System. Cynthia Zaitzevsky. The Belknap Press of Harvard University Press. 1982. (Paperback 1992) 262 pp.

Charles Eliot, Landscape Architect. Charles W. Eliot. Houghton Mifflin, Cambridge,1902. 770pp.

Cityscapes of Boston: An American City Through Time. Robert Campbell and Peter Vanderwarker, Houghton Mufflin Company, Boston 1992, 220 pp.

Lost Boston. Jane Holtz Kay. Houghton Mifflin Company. Boston. 1980. 304 pp.

Design on the Land: The Development of Landscape Architecture. Norman T. Newton. The Belknap Press of Harvard University. Cambridge. 1978. 714 pp.

AIA Guide to Boston, Second Edition. Susan and Michael Southworth. Globe Pequot Press, Old Saybrook, CT. 1992, 522 pp.

Boston, A Topographical History. Walter Muir Whitehill. Second Edition1968. The Belknap Press of Harvard University, Cambridge. 299 pp.

Frederick Law Olmsted: Designing the American Landscape. Charles E. Beveridge and Paul Rocheleau. Rizzoli, New York. 1995, 276 pp.

Christian Science Center

New England Natives: A Celebration of People and Trees, Sheila Connor. 1994. Harvard University Press, Cambridge. 274 pp.

So Fine a Prospect: Historic New England Gardens, Emmet, Alan. 1996. University Press of New England, Hanover, 230 pp.

"Image of a City," Bennett, Paul. Landscape Architecture Magazine, June 1999, p. 74-85, 102-107.

Additions, Corrections, Comments
Readers who believe an important site or project has been omitted from the guide or who have other comments or corrections are invited to submit them to the author for consideration in the next edition of this guidebook. Please respond to:

Jack Ahern, Professor
Department of Landscape Architecture and Regional Planning
University of Massachusetts
Amherst, MA 01003

Photo Credits

T = Top; M = Middle; B = Bottom; L = Left; C = Center; R = Right
Ahern, Jack: 1, 22TL, 27, 30B, 62T, 62B, 75T, 85T; Akiba, David: 12B, 35M, 35B, 37TR; Akiba, David/Sasaki Associates: 30M, 90; Bachelor, Clara: 25T, 25B; Blier, Michael, renderer/Hargreaves Associates: 17B; Boston Public Library: 24M; Brown and Rowe/Charles Mayer: 11B, 40T; Brown and Rowe: 49T ; Campbell, Gerry: 71; Childs, Bertman, Tseckares (CBT): 20T, 78; Central Artery/Tunnel Project Office: 9B, 21; Carol R. Johnson Associates/Jerry Howard: 22B, 47T, 48T, 60BR; Carol R. Johnson Associates: 10, 40B, 50B, 54, 56, 60BL, 61, 70, 72T, B. Cover, B.; Carrillo, Dixie: 63BL; Cortes Associates: 48B; Courtesy of the National Park Service, Frederick Law Olmsted National Historic Site: 34T, 36BL, 36BR, 38B, 41TR, 81; Davis, Michael: 69B; Del Tredici, Peter: 37TC, 37B; Earl R. Flansburgh and Associates: 19BR; Flannery, Mark C.: 23B; Fox, Tom: 55T, 57, 59B, 63T, 77; Grassl, Anton: 39B; Grassl, Anton/Pressley Associates: 8T; Horsman, Bill: 73; Howard, Jerry: 10T, 11T, 20B, 22TR, 44B, 49B, 79TL, 79TR, 84T; Isabella Stewart Gardner Museum: 29B; John Copley and Associates: 17T; Johnson, Ann: 28T; LaVallee, Robert: 69TL; Lynn Wolff Associates/John Copley Associates: 8B, 31, 34B, 35T, 46T, 46C, 51T, 81T, 85B; Lyon, Martha, Denig Design: 75B; MacLean, Alex /Landslides: Cover, 7T, 7B, 9T, 23T, 26T, 36T, 41B, 42, 45T, 47B, 66T, 67, 74T, 81B, 88T; Madsen, Karen: 37TL; Martin, John: 6, 58T, 63BR, 84B, 86T,86B, 87T; McCarthy, Walter: 69TR; MDC Archives: 68 ; Museum of Transportation: 50TR; Payne, Cymie: 18, 51B; Pressley, Marion: 29T; Pressley Associates: 59T; Rosenthal, Steve/Pressley Associates: 12T, 30T, 83T; Rosenthal, Steve: 51C; Sasaki Associates: 58B, 76, 88B; The Halvorson Company: 13B, 19MR, 28B, 29M, 38T, 39T, 39BC, 43, 44T, 55B, 83B, 87B, B.Cover, MR; The Massachusetts Archives: 26B, 80; Walker, Victor: 4, 19T, 24B, 24T, 34M, 41TL, 50TL, 52T, 52B, 74B B. Cover, T; Watkins, Ben E.: 19L, 46B, 55C; Vanderwalker, Peter/Pressley Associates: 13T, 16 B. Cover, BMR; Vanderwalker, Peter/The Halvorsen Company: 3; Wacker, John: 72B; Wallace Floyd: 66B, 79B; Weinreb, Stu.: 45C, 45B; Wheeler, Nick, Photographics: 52C.

Index of Projects by Firm/Designer and (Project Numbers)

Alphabetical Index of Projects and (Project Numbers)

Acknowledgments

Primary Financial support for this guidebook has been provided by:
The Hubbard Educational Trust,
John Wacker, President
The University of Massachusetts Amherst,
Department of Landscape Architecture and Regional Planning

Additional Financial Support Provided by:
Jestena Boughton, Colony Hotels, Delray Beach, Florida and Kennebunkport, Maine

The Hubbard Educational Trust, Guidebook Advisory Committee:
John F. Furlong
Carol R. Johnson
Marion Pressley
Lynn Wolff

The University of Massachusetts Project Team:
Karen Good, Project Manager
Kathleen Glasstetter, Assistant Editor
Jaiwei Wu, Map Design and Production

Design
Karen Chrisman, North Haven Design

Editor
Stephen Weldon, Chief Text Editor

Contributors and Reviewers
This project has been a collaborative effort involving literally hundreds of people, including students, professionals, public officials, and interested citizens. The list below is intended to be complete. The author accepts responsibility for any unintentional omissions.

Kathy Abbott, Boston Harbor Islands Alliance
Thomas Adams, John Wong, Tom Fox, SWA
Linda Ahern
Phyllis Andersen, The Arnold Arboretum
Fran Beatty and Cheri Ruane, Boston Parks Department
John Berg, Boston Community Gardeners
Shary Page Berg
Justin Berthiume, Moreice and Gary
Anthony Casendino, Casendino & Company
Dick Cohane, Boston Assessor's Office
John Copley, John Copley and Associates
Susan Child, Child Associates
Leslie Smith, Marion Pressley, Pressley Associates
Paula Cortes, Cortes Associates
Kate Diana, Dineen Crosby, Wallace Floyd Associates
Roger Erickson, Brighton CDC

Christopher Greene, The Halvorson Company
Frank Garnier, Olin Partnership
Margaret Gilligan, BSLA
Rolf Goetze, Boston Redevelopment Authority
Ann Gilardi Johnson
Erling "Bud" Hanson, Forest Hills Cemetery
Betsy Iglehart, Society for the Preservation of New England Antiquities
Sonja Johansson, Johansson & Walcavage
Robin Kanter
John Kissida, Camp, Dresser and McKee
Patrice Kish and Katie Lacy, Massachusetts Department of Environmental Management
Claire Lane
Martha Lyon, Denig Design Associates
John Martin, University of Massachusetts
Kaki Martin, Mark Klopfer, Hargraeves Associates
Shirley Muirhead, Boston Redevelopment Authority
Lauren Meier, National Park Service
Julia O'Brien, Karl Haglund, Sean Fisher and Dan Driscoll, Metropolitan District Commission
Teresa Gray Pierce, Kerri Purrini, Sasaki Associates
Ellen Rahr, ASLA
Clarissa Rowe, Shirley Kressel, Emilie Stuart, Brown and Rowe
Kathy Sharkey, Massachusetts Horticultural Society
Melanie Simo
Francis Fox Spinks
Mary Alice Van Sickle, Tom Doolittle, Carol Johnson, Carol R. Johnson Associates, Inc.
John Wacker, Wacker Associates
Victor Walker, Walker-Kleussing Design Group
Wesley Ward, Michael Triff, The Trustees of Reservations
Stu Weinreb
Pam Whitley, Mary Smith Associates
Lynn Wolff, Lynn Wolff Associates Inc.
Cynthia Zaitzevsky, Cynthia Zaitzevsky Associates
Mark Zarillo, Symmes, Maini & McKee

University of Massachusetts, Department of Landscape Architecture and Regional Planning Students:
Rebecca Bacchand, Stephen Bagley, Jason Bobowski, Sue Brown, Tony Cowles, Kat Hardesty, Adam Hubbard, Katie Lalibertie, Kathleen Lessard, Luisa Olivera, Scott Roe, Isobel Roy, Karen Sebastian.

Printer
Thames Printing Company, Norwich, CT

Binding
Mueller Trade Bindery, Middletown, CT

Film
Atlantic Digital Images, Latham, NY